Demolishing Myths or Mosques and Temples?

Demolishing Myths or Mosques and Temples?

Readings on History and Temple Desecration in Medieval India

Edited with an Introduction by

Sunil Kumar

Three Essays
COLLECTIVE

First Edition April 2008
Reprint January 2025

ISBN 978-81-88789-59-7

Three Essays
COLLECTIVE

B-957 Palam Vihar, GURGAON (Haryana) 122 017 India
Phone: 91-124 2369023, +91 98681 26587, +91 98683 44843
info@threeessays.com Website: www.threeessays.com
Printed at Replika Press Pvt Ltd, India

For my father, Shri Naresh Kumar,
whose ideals of humanity and social justice
will always remain an inspiration.

Contents

Contributors

Richard Davis teaches at Bard College. Previous publications include: *Ritual in an Oscillating Universe: Worshipping Śiva in Medieval India;* ed., *Images, Miracles and Authority in Asian Religious Traditions*; and *Lives of Indian Images*.

Romila Thapar is Emeritus Professor of History, Jawaharlal Nehru University. A selection of her publications would include: *Aśoka and the Decline of the Mauryas; Early India; Ancient Indian Social History: Some Interpretations; From Lineage to State; History and Beyond; Cultural Pasts: Essays in Early Indian History; Śakuntalā: Texts, Readings, Histories* and *Somanātha: the Many Voices of a History.*

Richard Eaton teaches at the University of Arizona, Tucson. Previous publications include: *Sufis of Bijapur 1300-1700: Social Roles of Sufis in Medieval India; Rise of Islam and the Bengal Frontier; Essays on Islam and Indian History;* ed., *India's Islamic Traditions;* and (with George Michell) *Firuzabad: Palace City of the Deccan*.

Finbarr Barry Flood teaches at New York University. Previous publications include: *The Great Mosque of Damascus: Studies on the Making of an Umayyad Visual Culture*, several articles and the forthcoming titles: *The Materials of Translation: Subjects and Objects in the first Indo-Persian Polity*, and *Altered Images: Islam, Iconoclasm, and the Mutability of Meaning*.

Sunil Kumar is professor of medieval history in the Department of History, Delhi University. His previous publications include *The Present in Delhi's Pasts* and *The Emergence of the Delhi Sultanate*. He has also participated in the current revision of the NCERT history textbooks and is the managing editor of the *Indian Economic and Social History Review*.

The editor is grateful to the respective authors for permission to reprint their articles. He would also like to thank Richard Davis and Finbarr Barry Flood for providing the photographs that accompany their contributions. A special mention needs to be made of the American Institute of Indian Studies, Delhi and of Shantilal Nanjibhai Bhatt, Bhatt Art Studio, Datar Road, Junagadh for permission to use their photographs. Precise acknowledgements are included in the captions that follow the illustrations.

I have made no attempt to introduce consistency in the diacritical method and bibliographic systems followed by the different authors. For the better part, the form of the original publication has been retained.

Introduction

December 6, 1992 ... the day a sixteenth century mosque was demolished. A day that carries a vignette of images: youths dancing on the domes of the Babri masjid, cudgeling it to rubble, national politicians haranguing the congregation on to greater hatred and violence, policemen standing by as mute spectators and journalists threatened and manhandled. These snapshots do not do justice, however, to the atrocity that was December 6, 1992.

To capture the true implications of its horror we have to scroll back a few years to 1990 and the *Rath Yatra*, the ceremonial procession of the Bharatiya Janata Party (BJP) president Lal Krishan Advani. In an effort to mobilise electoral support Mr Advani appeared as the champion of Lord Rama. Advani's yatra invoked a reading of history where it was claimed that Mīr Bāqī, a commander of the first Mughal emperor, Babur (r. 1526-30), destroyed a temple consecrating the site of Lord Rama's birth. Babur and his military commander profaned the sacred area, the Ramjanmabhumi, by constructing a mosque on the site of the temple. This grievous injury to the sentiment of the Hindu community was intolerable and, nearly six centuries after the event, the BJP and its president made the restitution of past wrongs to the Hindu community a central agenda in their political manifesto. Mr Advani's yatra traversed several states in north India spreading its message of hatred and spite, urging people to greater self-pride, mobilising them in a war to protect their culture, their religion, their state. Indeed, Advani's yatra quickly transcended from election rhetoric to a full-fledged campaign against the secular modern state of India. It was a battle against the incumbent government and all others in the past who did not demolish Babur's offensive mosque on the Ramjanmabhumi. Advani and his peers argued that secular sentiments only pampered the minority community even as they trampled Hindu pride. The yatra was therefore a 'liberation struggle', led by Mr Advani astride his festooned Toyota chariot, a caricature of Rama's mythic battle against the anti-hero, Ravana, a Hindu nationalism that was majoritarian and blatantly militant in character.

In its wake, Advani's yatra spread violence and divisiveness. The country experienced some of the worst communal conflicts of the century in 1990. But this was only the beginning.

Scroll forward some weeks beyond December 1992 and the destruction of the Babri masjid by cadres and volunteers (*kar sevaks*) brought to Ayodhya by the BJP and its associates, the Vishwa Hindu Parishad (VHP) and the Rashtriya Swayamsevak Sangh (RSS). Even as Advani celebrated the destruction of the mosque that had brought him such significance as a national politician, communal riots burned the country for two months. Through the months of December and January 1992-3, communal conflict left over 3,000 dead. Within a week, conservative estimates put 600 people killed in Bombay alone. Women and children were hunted down in the streets; domiciles and business establishments left smoldering for days. Countless were left homeless, orphaned, widowed and raped. They remained anonymous, part of no official statistics, their trauma presumably insignificant in a historical frame that shifted very quickly to the utopia of a destined *Ram-rajya*.

Over fifteen years have passed since the events of December 6th 1992. Much has transpired in the interim. Lal Krishan Advani was, for a while, the Deputy Prime Minister of India and, quite ironically for a person who broke his pledge to the Supreme Court and exhorted *kar sevak*s to destroy the mosque, also the country's Home Minister. The BJP used its term in office (1999-2004) to consolidate its recent electoral gains. Hindutva mobilization during the last two decades of the past millennium – their inroads into the public domain and the global nexus of many of these developments – has been the subject of considerable research, not least of all by authors writing in the Readings published by the Three Essays Collective. If there is any common thread running amidst this body of writing, it is the warning that the conflagration in Gujarat in the spring of 2002 was not an aberration: the methodical planning, the killing of minority groups, violence perpetrated on women and children were all a part of a cynical agenda at ethnic-cleansing, the move to terrorise minorities and create a homogenous, majoritarian society by Hindutva agencies. Yet, although the systematic violence perpetrated on the Muslim population in Gujarat was a pogrom, aided and abetted by a collusive state machinery, it was successful in its electoral goals. Hindutva mobilization in Gujarat was successful enough in translating these macabre events into a huge victory during the 2003 and 2007 state elections. Repelling as it may sound, it was not surprising that these electoral gains were seen by Hindutva forces as a vindication of their methods of social engineering.

These were disquieting trends: where repulsive violence and murder could be tolerated, even exonerated, in the cause of purifying the body politic. No one factor can help explain these developments and certainly a study of the short duration can only help us understand the manner in which some of these processes consolidated and enabled Hindutva successes. Take, for example, the challenge to India's secular identity through ongoing efforts to rationalise the reading of the country's past along communal lines. Even as professional scholars have discarded the nineteenth century colonial trifurcation of Indian history into Hindu, Muslim and the British periods because of its racial, religious and colonial presuppositions, new and even more pernicious ideologies are reintroducing these modes of interpretation in the public realm.

I say 'reintroducing' because the impact of communal sensibilities on the interpretation of Indian history is a long one in which a variety of different people were involved. In the context of colonial critiques of a moribund, effete Indian civilisation, the writings of some early nationalists in the late nineteenth century represent one strand. They wanted to create a national identity, a history that represented the glories of the subcontinent's past, a narrative that could unite its multi-cultural complexity. They could do this in many ways, but one unhappy choice centred upon the identification of 'heroes' whose actions could inspire a new generation of patriotic Indians. As a result they wrote histories, popular stories and plays, valorising the conduct of heroes such as Prithviraj Chauhan, Shivaji and Rana Pratap. The early nationalists wanted to indoctrinate a new generation of Indians to fight courageously against their British colonial oppressors, to learn about patriotism and nationalism from the life stories of these immortal personalities. And they were enormously successful: the evocative stories of these heroes had a huge circulation. Many of their more patriotic epics are still included in history and Hindi textbooks of school children. What is ignored in the retelling of these histories is the manner in which their narratives led generations of children into assuming that Hindus and Indians were congruent categories. Or the manner in which these stories juxtaposed protagonists: Hindus/Indians were the ones who bravely resisted the foreign/Muslim invaders, aliens who colonised India in an earlier period. Successive generations of Indian citizens were reared under the belief that to be proud of one's nation meant that one was equally proud of being a Hindu, and patriotism meant resisting both, British and Muslim aggression. It also helped to consolidate the seriously flawed impression that

'Hindus' are a monolithic religious and social community, the subcontinent's primordial residents. Conversely Muslims are almost universally regarded as a monolithic group, foreigners to India because of their history and alien culture.

These nineteenth and early twentieth century ideas were nurtured in history textbooks, popular literature and the media, until they came to possess a commonsensical validity that was rarely subjected to critical interrogation. It was in an attempt to curb the dissemination of these sentiments that the Indian government, still inspired by its socialistic, secular Nehruvian ideals, decided to produce textbooks that were 'scientifically oriented' so that they could provide an objective, secular interpretation of Indian history. The task was given to the National Council of Educational Research and Training (NCERT), a nodal body responsible for the development of school curricula and pedagogical enhancement in the country.

Given the level of underdevelopment and poverty, the vast social and ideological complexities surrounding questions of literacy, gender emancipation, racial, caste and religious prejudices through the 1960s and 70s, a proactive role of the state in the affairs of education was welcome. Certainly the history textbooks of the time were written by professional historians whose eminence in their respective fields was universally recognized. Their historiographies reflected an emphasis on economic determinism and class struggles, a means to move beyond hero-centred and religious-community based interpretations. A good beginning, perhaps, but barring minor updates, these texts remained in circulation for nearly two decades!

When the NDA government came to power, the BJP controlled the ministries that governed the nation's educational and cultural policies. Institutions like the University Grants Commission (UGC), the Indian Council of Historical Research (ICHR), the Indian Council for Cultural Relations (ICCR) and the Archaeological Survey of India (ASI) were staffed with either BJP cadres or individuals whose 'pragmatic' ideologies allowed for an easy collaboration with the BJP regime in exchange for career advancement. Indeed, patronage politics may have had a long institutional history in post-independence India but the goals of the BJP, propelled as it was by its saffron agencies, should never be forgotten. More than ever before, the acquisition of power provided the BJP with the opportunity to financially sponsor and direct public reflection on questions of identity and social relations from a majoritarian Hindu perspective.

Under the BJP regime, school curricula was revamped and history textbooks rewritten. Normally this is a useful, important exercise where recent historiographical trends can be incorporated in school texts and students introduced to the basics of the discipline. The garnering of additional or different 'facts' and details alone is ordinarily not a part of this exercise. Instead, rewriting history textbooks implies rethinking how the discipline of history can be conveyed to young minds. It involves an attempt to introduce students to the kinds of evidence used by historians in their research. These texts should try to debate different ways of reading evidence; carry the excitement of new horizons in historical research opened up by archaeology, art history and literature; warn students about the problems of anachronistic and teleological reasoning in history. In other words, rather than a rote learning of arcane information, greater attention to how and why historians select their 'facts' and weave them into their arguments would teach students more about history than an evaluation of the qualities of a 'classical age' or the reasons for the 'decline of an empire'.

How do social, political and economic processes, for example, structure and shape life? How are ideologies and beliefs constructed by both, subaltern classes and dominant elites, sometimes as resistance to class oppression? In what ways do master-narratives of imperial formations make the writing of regional, class and gender sensitive histories difficult? Is the study of change intrinsic to history? Historians today are studying these questions in interesting and innovative ways but it should hardly surprise us that the revised history textbooks eschewed debates or the processes of historical inquiry. They instead provided 'facts' and the ones that they choose to stress – and ignore – were significant.

According to the revised NCERT textbooks 'facts' proved that Indian civilisation sprang fully formed – caste system, cow worship, et al. – in the Vedic age, at the dawn of global civilisation, circa 2500 BC or earlier. They teach that the dharmashastras and other brahmanical normative texts with a limited circulation were instead the legal digests that shaped life and political constitutions of the ancient Indian regimes. This is now marked as India's heritage, one that students need to honour and cherish. In other words, together with the Vedas, Hinduism had its genesis at the dawn of time, and this religion governed every facet of life in a period that should correctly be described as the 'Hindu Period' of Indian history. Students were asked to memorise facts that confirm how a sacred, becalmed, unchanging golden age of the ancient world suffered only one, serious, traumatic dislocation: the coming of Islam and Muslims into the subcontinent. This 'foreign' religion and its followers corrupted the pristine Vedic world of the Hindus and introduced traditions like purdah, dowry and cow slaughter.

The demolition of the Babri masjid and Hindutva mobilization through the 1990s, its attack upon the discipline of history and the increasing communal polarisation of Indian society was strongly challenged by professional historians of a variety of ideological spectrums. It led to the production of some fascinating research in social history, religion, gender studies, nationalism, the history of ideas and caste, all of which complicated simple-minded renditions of history that juxtaposed monolithic communities in perpetual conflict. Unfortunately, much of this recent work circulates within the walls of the academy: professional historians writing for their colleagues and research students. Not enough of this work has penetrated into the realm of school textbooks. With the sole exception of some vernacular presses, many with leftist sympathies, the public domain is still prey to 'pulp history' that narrates the past within simple binary templates: heroes versus villains; the virtuous against the immoral and the nationalist Hindu in conflict with the foreign Muslim or British forces.

The collection of essays in this volume hopes to bridge the serious gap between historical research available in the academy and the materials accessible to school and college teachers, students and other interested readers. It is hoped that this compilation of essays by historians will help secular minded Indians formulate their ideas with greater confidence and coherence and make others doubt their first assumptions.

The theme of temple desecration and destruction in the medieval period was deliberately chosen for this book because the subject has a direct bearing upon the Babri Masjid-Ramjanmabhumi issue, a subject that has divided the country for so many years and shed so much blood. Much of the literature on the Babri Masjid-Ramjanmabhumi issue has centred on the validity or weakness in the claims of the various litigants. For many people the controversy has now whittled down to the pivotal question: was there an ancient Ram temple on the site of Babur's (demolished) mosque? The subject is now pending before the Supreme Court. As a part of its efforts to resolve the controversy the Supreme Court ordered the Archaeological Survey of India (ASI) to ascertain whether there were any prior constructions under the now demolished Babri Masjid.

From a variety of different perspectives, this was a baffling intervention. The Indian subcontinent has one of the longest histories of human settlements in the world and excavations in most places have revealed layers upon layers of human habitation, sometimes stretching beyond the last two millennia. Of all the different types of material remains, that may hypothetically remain buried under the site of the demolished mosque, why is a Hindu temple singled out as an object of such interest? Indeed, even though the site was considerably disturbed, excavations at the Babri Masjid site revealed the evidence of early habitation and material remains from a variety of different time periods. Some artefacts were identified rather ambiguously as belonging to the early medieval period and the Archaeological Survey of India (ASI) suggested that they indicated the presence of a large construction. The nature of these artefacts, not least their precise temporal contexts, were difficult to determine with any sense of accuracy. Following a comparative methodology, the ASI concluded that these were in the nature of materials belonging to a huge temple from the early medieval period.

The evidence was hardly equivocal on this point. Other archaeologists who also studied the evidence suggested that the artefacts on the basis of which the ASI postulated the presence of a huge temple were not the bases of pillars at all. Doubts arose from the quality of the remains, their grid locations and the stratographic levels at which they were discovered. Perhaps, even more telling was their criticism regarding the selective study of data by the ASI, the manner in which some parts of the evidence were highlighted and other parts diluted. Some evidence was recorded in the ASI report only after independent observers on the site protested at their exclusion. The motivated nature of the excavations and the biases in its report were further underlined by the extremely inconsistent chronological methods followed by the Survey. Were some of the discovered artefacts from the Sultanate period or earlier? In the context of the 'Hindu-Muslim' binarism that was guiding the whole inquiry this was hardly a small issue. The manner in which the ASI report glossed over data inconvenient to its larger conclusions hardly reassured critics of its impartial conduct in the inquiry.

The debate around the Ramjanmabhumi/Babri masjid issue and the report of the Archaeological Survey actually underscored the paucity of historical and archaeological information available to conclude with any certainty whether a temple existed on the site of the demolished mosque. If anything, the ambiguous results of the Archaeological Survey of India excavations have provided material to contending parties to argue their respective cases even more vociferously. In the interim however, by getting the ASI involved in this debate, the Supreme Court has succeeded in forever tarnishing the institution's reputation; for many, the Survey's Hindutva biases are now confirmed.

But beyond these debates are the larger questions that the Supreme Court seems to have ignored. Not the least of which pertain to the disciplines of history and archaeology that were deployed to provide facts for a case under litigation. Puranic histories, epic tales and decontextualised material remains of uncertain provenance are not the sources with which historians or archaeologists can answer questions posed by present day politicians. Certainly the nature of the debate itself lends to a presentist reading of the past, a teleology that is methodologically suspect for its selective sifting of facts to suit divergent political arguments. This is a method that professional historians and archaeologists would eschew in the practice of their trade. But thanks to the Supreme Court decision to use the Archaeological Survey of India as a detective agency it is exactly these scholastic traditions of social science research that are now under threat.

In its search for facts to ascertain whether the Babri masjid was constructed on the site of a Hindu temple, the Supreme Court seems to have completely ignored the central question: can an event that supposedly transpired in the sixteenth century be treated as a grievance and redressed in the twenty-first? Will the desecration of Vaishnavite temples by Shaivites or the destruction of Buddhist sacred places by a variety of Hindu agencies be judged by the same yardstick? It is significant that Hindutva ideologues have now started arguing that the Supreme Court verdict notwithstanding, the Ramjanmabhumi temple will be constructed. Hindu religious and emotional sentiments demand this; the state, its courts and the country's constitution are peripheral to the issue! The clamour of demographic numbers implies that majoritarian sentiments should now definitively determine policy. Neither history nor archaeology is actually pertinent in this argument and Indians can never remain confident where the search for restitution of past injury will take the nation next. Are Mathura and Kashi included amongst the places awaiting 'liberation'? Will the 'recapturing' of sites lost in some mythic past also legitimize the destruction of neighbourhood Sufi shrines as in Gujarat in 2002? What criteria are we going to use to construct our history of grievances and whom are we appointing to undertake this task for us?

* * *

The essays in this volume do not engage with the Babri masjid-Ramjanmabhumi controversy directly. They however pick up several issues integral to the manner in which debates around this episode are framed. The first essay in this collection by Richard Davis studies the question of looting temples and discusses its meanings within the medieval context of state formation and conquest. In a startling departure from the 'commonsensical' take on Indian history where the looting and desecration of Hindu temples is always associated with Muslim invaders, Davis studies the looting of temples carried out by 'Hindu' Rajas. It is little known that victorious Hindu Rajas pillaged the temples of their vanquished rivals, looted their idols and installed them as war trophies in their own temples. The systematic practice of this iconoclasm and plunder of each other's temples by Hindu rulers was integral to their claims of universal lordship bestowed by God. Davis's work makes the crucial point that warfare and looting were adjuncts to the constitution of medieval political authority. 'Looting' cannot be interpreted through modern filters as a disruption of a stable political and moral order. Instead we need to remember that the later constructed Lakshman temple in Khajuraho was specially commissioned by the Candella Raja Yaśovarman to house the solid-gold Viṣṇu statue he had looted from the Pratihara rulers. The looting and desecration of a competitor's deity, its reinstallation by the conqueror in his own temple were important public declarations of the defeat of an old ruler and the arrival of a new political lord and master of the region.

The practice of looting and desecrating temples of political competitors was an important aspect in the construction of a dominant political formation. This was as true for victorious Hindu rulers, as it was for Muslim ones in the Middle Ages. Equally, if the looting of temples was a part of a more general pre-modern political culture – the religious denomination of the ruler notwithstanding — then the question of restitution of past grievances is impossible to pursue. Central to Davis's study is the manner in which modern historians should comprehend medieval practices of authority and conquest. What are the skills required in translating and communicating medieval lexicons of power into modern historical narratives? Or, turning the question around, one could also ask about the nature of modern filters that guide our interpretation of pre-modern political conduct in India from such a biased perspective. Why is it that iconoclasm and temple desecration is so universally associated with Muslims in our history textbooks and the popular imagination? Why are we so universally uninformed about the more general phenomenon of temple desecration carried out by Medieval rulers, Hindus and Muslims alike?

Romila Thapar's article on the destruction of the temple of Somnath by Mahmud of Ghazni addresses this question squarely. Historians generally describe the destruction of this temple as an event of cataclysmic proportions that marked the onset of the Muslim/Medieval period and with it the start of a routine desecration of Hindu temples by Muslims. These events were reported in the Persian chronicles of the Delhi Sultans and Mughal Padishahs and often the evidence of ruined temples is still visible to modern visitors. For many historians, therefore, Islamic iconoclasm was not a subject worthy of further investigation; it was an inescapable fact.

Romila Thapar's work, however, questions the 'evidence' that supports these assumptions. She studies the manner in which different narratives of the destruction of Somnath were written. Contrary to received opinion, the author explains, the Somnath temple was not an important site of worship for Hindus in the tenth century. As Romila Thapar points out, the importance of the temple of Somnath was, quite ironically, the creation of Persian historians who were the ones to suggest that it was a pivotal religious centre for Hindus in India. This helped to burnish Mahmud of Ghazni's reputation as the non-pariel iconoclastic destroyer of his time and for later authors, a rhetorical trope that could function as a paradigm of Muslim sovereignty in India. The Persian narrativisation of the Somnath expedition was, however, only one of several accounts; there were several other interesting ways in which this event was also redeployed. Jain authors, for instance, claimed the destruction of the Somnath temple as a proof of the superior power of Jainism over Saivism: Mahavir protected Jain temples while Siva remained powerless to protect his adherents.

In the nineteenth and twentieth centuries British and later nationalist historians further burnished the image of Somnath, not just as a central icon within a Hindu geography of sacred sites, but as a symbol of India's injured pride that needed restoration. Ironically the British colonial regime was the first to don the mantle of restorer of Indian/Hindu pride, a sentiment that was appropriated by some nationalist leaders in the twentieth century. The complex past of Somnath was completely erased by a nationalist pride that re-consecrated a newly constructed temple on the site in 1951 and restored Indian/Hindu honour. As Romila Thapar points out in her essay, rather than the 'facts' surrounding Somnath it is the manner in which the event was historicised at selective stages of its past that provides it with the national significance it carries in our memory today. And let us not forget, in 1990 Lal Krishan Advani deliberately evoked only one aspect of the past when he started his Rath yatra to Ayodhya from Somnath.

The modern experience of communal conflict and partition certainly directs our concern to questions of community consciousness, identity formation and conflict in the pre-modern period. These are important questions but as the research of Davis and Thapar suggests, the pre-history of modern sensibilities are sometimes so distant from us today that we need to study them as if we were engaging with an unfamiliar culture. Learning the language and the grammar of the texts that report on past social practices and beliefs provides historians with the skills to discover the complex manner in which 'reality' was constructed by a variety of mediating agencies: religious and historical texts, art, architecture and so on. Reading the past from this perspective means that we cannot simply depend upon the evidence of 'reliable sources' but have to interrogate them and carry out our own independent investigation. This could lead historians to conclusions that do not support a variety of apriori assumptions. Certainly, as the work of Davis and Thapar points out, a careful reading of past evidence disturbs central assumptions that we carry with us without any further reflection. Muslim iconoclasm, the importance of Somnath for Hindus are ahistoricised assumptions that help in fashioning the sense of a Hindu India where Muslims are violent intruders. The genealogy supporting the history of grievance is remarkably weak and one-sided.

But this is also the reason why the discipline of history cannot be used to support presentist ultra-nationalist political agendas. It is also the reason why so much historical research is violently attacked today and denied circulation. We cannot suffer the thought that 'Indians' in the Vedic age – the great 'Aryans' themselves – ate beef! The historian that suggested this must be anti-nationalist. He and his work must be violently condemned. Simple narratives that provide linear connections with the great traditions of the past are, on the other hand, touted as veritable truths. As we search for our identities in a post-colonial world, the Ramayana and the Mahabharata suddenly emerge as vivid images through which we can construct national and family traditions. The NCERT textbooks of the NDA regime are culpable in the circulations of these ideologies. What we need instead is a more intensive, transparent debate about the manner in which we construct our histories, a discussion of the sources that historians use (and ignore) and the methods that they deploy towards their analysis.

The third essay in this collection, by Richard Eaton, engages with the debate surrounding temple desecration very directly. To begin with, Eaton sifts through the most commonly cited sources supporting the general assumption that Muslims desecrated Hindu temples. Eaton tabled the information regarding the desecration of temples chronologically and then mapped the evidence geographically. His conclusions were fascinating. Rather than reporting a random record of Muslim iconoclasm, there was a clear pattern of temple desecration across hostile frontiers as invading armies faced resistance. Alternatively, temple desecration took place during revolts. Eaton also asked if Muslims were inherently iconoclastic: did they, in other words, desecrate all temples? His research suggested otherwise. Only temples constructed by royal patrons or their political agents were desecrated.

Eaton's investigation confirmed Davis' research: royal temples were public arenas where imperial authority was ritually legitimated and hierarchical relationships with subordinate chieftains consolidated through a variety of transactional relationships. The defeat of a ruler provoked the public humiliation of his 'signs' of authority by the victorious army. This was a part of the culture of power and authority that was enacted in different ways by both, Hindu and Muslim rulers in the medieval period. Only royal temples during moments of conflict were desecrated. By contrast, temples that did not 'challenge' the regnant authority were protected as state-property and their continued patronage was evidence of the universal justice that righteous kings claimed was maintained in their realm. This was an accolade that Muslim rulers cherished and often received from their 'Hindu' subjects, 'facts' not commonly known and certainly absent in NCERT textbooks or BJP rhetoric. Certainly, once temple desecration is placed within the context of medieval kingship and the consecration of royal authority it no longer appears as evidence of irrational, fanatical, religious bigotry. Both Hindu and Muslim rulers comprehended its political and religious iconography and its enactment had a very precise historical context.

The need to emphasise the historical context to understand the nature of iconoclasm was also stated by Barry Flood, the author of the fourth essay in this volume. Flood, an art historian, queried the notion of Islamic iconoclasm and asked the simple question: are Muslims the same everywhere through all periods of time? The answer was an obvious, no! Flood further asked: if the quality of being a Muslim was historically and regionally determined, then how historically sensitive were general ascriptions of Muslims as pathologically iconoclastic fanatics? Surely the nature of iconoclasm was touched by a variety of contingent historical factors and not just a general Weberian Muslim one?

This was a line of interrogation very close to the one followed by Eaton but Flood revisited the question of 'Islamic' iconoclasm by a review of Ghurid aesthetics. As he argued, Ghurid aesthetics were strongly impressed with Indic decorative forms. The masjid-i sangi at Larvand in Afghanistan decorated with vase-and-foliage capitals, lotus scrolls and half-lotus friezes underscored the positive aesthetic value attached by the Ghurids to standard decorative elements of Indic architecture. In Flood's argument, this aesthetic was also apparent in the iconoclasm practiced by the Ghurids in India. Rather than a generic 'Islamic' iconoclasm, Flood suggested, study the materials destroyed or defaced so that we can better appreciate the choices made by the iconoclasts. Flood studied the evidence of the Qutb mosque in Delhi and placed it in the larger context of Ghurid architecture in Afghanistan and north India. Barring a few exceptions, anthropomorphic imagery was mutilated in the mosque but other representational forms, including figural imagery – also forbidden in Islam – was left untouched. This included elephants, birds and mythological creatures such as maqaras and the kirtimukha, the horned lion, which 'became as ubiquitous a figure [in Ghurid mosques in north India] as it had been in pre-Ghurid Buddhist stupas and Hindu temples'. In other words, the Qutb witnessed a selective iconoclasm, one that was motivated by a deliberate choice that left intact figural representation that the Ghurids preferred aesthetically.

Taken together with Eaton's arguments, Flood's research points to the importance of moving away from easy interpretations of 'random and fanatic Muslim iconoclasm' to a more nuanced analysis of the agencies involved in the event. The desecration of temples was a deliberate event enacted by victorious Hindu and Muslim rulers over vanquished kings and rebels. But as Flood suggests we can carry the study of desecration further. There was an appreciation of decorative styles and imagery that spanned what we today refer to as juxtaposed and homogenized 'Hindu and Muslim' worlds and this inflected the direction and extent of desecration of idols. Flood makes the additional point that the study of iconoclasm is prefigured within an ahistorical, synchronic universe, where the destructive as well as the creative impulse is removed from the processes of artistic creation and recreation. While today we can only bemoan the mutilated idol, Flood suggests a rereading of the iconoclastic moment as a tranformative one where a new aesthetic was represented. This is evident if we study the Qutb mosque as a unitary whole where it is virtually impossible to extract despoliated elements from the newer materials. Just as the Candella Raja's Lakshman temple in Khajuraho is not remembered today as a site constructed to house the looted Viṣṇu statue of the Pratihara rulers, the creative energies deployed at the moment of reconstruction in the Qutb mosque also need to be appreciated outside the genealogy of grievance that has completely seized our historical imagination.

The essays of Davis, Thapar, Eaton and Flood also touch upon 'religion' and 'politics' in overlapping ways. Although they do not explicitly discuss it in their essays, it is clear that when they talk about 'religion' they refer not merely to organized belief systems, but also to the texts, rituals, art forms and public arenas where they were re-produced. In an important sense, 'religion' for these authors was not merely a life-orientational idea that transcended a material reality, but an ideology that had a sacred resonance with an identifiable material context. And because it was more than personal piety – an individual's search for absolute truth – religion's organizational aspect, its changing institutional form, was a crucial subject of historical inquiry. All the essays in this book cover a time period spanning the 8th through the 18th centuries of the Common Era, a thousand years of enormous change in the complexion of religion and social organizations. These were the years of political empowerment of a variety of marginalized groups, when pastoralists and low-caste warriors seized authority and established their separate dynasties all over the subcontinent. These were centuries of considerable political conflict when authority was constantly challenged by new aspirants. Brief moments of political stability were celebrated: temples were built, grants disbursed to religious elites and eulogies in praise of new and relatively unknown political masters narrated in inscriptions and texts.

The construction of the grand medieval temple, in other words, was related to the new political and social organizations that emerging political groups and their collaborators wanted to endow with moral sanctity. Their desecration was intrinsic to the ongoing process of political and social change characteristic of this time period. Those who had vested interests in preserving an old order, not surprisingly, produced much of the literature of the period that bemoaned the character of this change. The pastoralists, or the groups that eventually proclaimed themselves as Rajputs, hardly had reason to abhor the cataclysmic events that brought them to power. But once they were in power they condemned threats to their authority by demons and foreigners even as they suggested a primordial, divine right to authority. The irony behind these ascriptions should not be missed; in another context and at an earlier time period, some of these parvenu warriors were described by the power of the day as barbarians and agents that introduced the *kali-yug*.

Temple-desecration, then, is of great significance for the entry that it provides us into questions of medieval social, political, and religious organizations, into the manner in which authority and social hierarchies were constructed, legitimated, torn down or redeployed in the Middle Ages. These are exciting questions regarding historical change through which social structures in the subcontinent were reinvented, a dialectic that was integral to the processes that shaped our modern history. We can remain trapped with memories of injury and grievance only if we rather surreally identify with the protagonists involved in the conflicts that raged in the subcontinent a thousand years ago. And we can only do so by completely decontextualising the conflict and ourselves, by inhabiting a 'Wonderland' where somebody like L. K. Advani can imagine for a moment that he is Rama's avenger in combat with the generals of the Mughal emperor Babur! This is political rhetoric not history and it deserves as much credence as the American President's claims to represent the forces of civilization in a just war against the evil state of Iraq.

Political rhetoric, however, attempts to gain credence through its own deployment of 'history', a practice that we need to recognize for its presentist, motivated agendas. In contrast to the four essays by professional historians, the appendix to this book is not by a historian, but by an individual who frequently deploys the past to mobilize political opinion and rationalize the actions of his party-members. The former Prime Minister of India, Atal Bihari Vajpayee, is a savant, not just a politician of considerable experience but a poet whose nuanced speeches are very rich in their allusions to the past and how they reflect on the present. In the Appendix of this volume is the text of a speech that he delivered at Somnath on October 31st, 2001, on the fiftieth anniversary of the reconstruction of the temple.

In it the Prime Minister recalled how Somnath was an example of 'our' sanatan dharma, 'our' pure [brahmanical] culture, 'our' shashwat dharma, 'our' eternal culture. He noticed that it was an example of the continuous change present in Indian history. India and Somnath both faced foreign invasions in the past. Somnath was destroyed, but the Prime Minister noted that just as 'we' rebuilt Somnath, made a new Somnath and triumphed over those that sought to destroy it, we will also be victorious over terrorists who do not want to worship idols but destroy them. Vajpayee's speech was brilliantly crafted for its recourse to several overlapping illusions: a pure, brahmanical timeless civilisation of India, a civilisation where Somnath and India were synonymous, where both faced foreign invasions, Muslim invaders in the past who were seamlessly transported into the present as terrorists who challenged India's integrity. The rebuilding of the modern nation along its original dharmic ideals was captured in the history of the ruined Somnath temple. Somnath was an example of the challenges India had faced in the past and the rebuilt temple and pilgrimage centre was a sign of a new united India that was honest to its cultural past and committed to modernity and progress. In the Prime Minister's speech old nationalist leaders like Sardar Vallabhai Patel who had championed the cause of temple reconstruction in Somnath were appropriated within the Hindutva fold. Somnath and Gujarat, ruled by the BJP, gestured towards a Hindu imagination of a new India. Temple desecration was an event in the past and temple restoration was marked as the symbol of a new, proud, Hindu nation.

But what messages does this speech carry regarding the history of India, leave alone its secular character? Gujarat burnt not longer than five months after the Prime Minister's speech. Muslims were branded as foreigners and, as traitors, many were publicly executed. The perpetrators of this violence were not just provoked by an incident, the torching of a train carriage and the murder of its passengers. Their hatred was directed to a whole body of people of a certain religion who they regarded as cultural and social 'foreigners' to their understanding of 'India'. This was a deep-rooted belief, sustained and developed by a reading of history that validated the fissures amongst Indians and provoked hatred and incredible violence. It led to widespread mistrust and suspicion, sentiments that were not created by an 'event' but by a series of public interventions wherein the characterization of the past played an extremely important role. By contrasting Atal Bihari Vajpayee's speech with the work of professional historians it is hoped that the readers of this volume will never confuse political rhetoric with history and at the same time comprehend the huge power that history does possess to shape the destiny of the nation today. It also means that we have to function more responsibly as critical consumers of the past, an ongoing effort where I hope the essays in this volume will prove helpful.

INDIAN ART OBJECTS AS LOOT*

RICHARD H. DAVIS

Let us imagine a graceful bronze image of Dancing Śiva before us. It was perhaps created by a Cola artist in eleventh-century Tamilnadu to be installed in a temple to receive offerings of worship, and to parade around the town in a ceremonial palanquin on festival days. From there, this image might have followed any of several paths to stand before us now in a North American museum. Perhaps it was buried under a banyan tree in late fourteenth century when invading Islamic armies, feared for their iconoclasm, marched through the Kaveri delta on their way to Madurai. It could have been disinterred in the nineteenth century, during British rule, by a Tamil workman on a road crew, who showed it to the civil engineer, who brought it to the attention of the District Collector, who passed it on to the Director of Archaeology. In the twentieth century, perhaps, when an international market developed for such objects, it might have ended up in an auction room, a cosmic dance sold to the highest bidder. Or a government expert on culture might have selected it, after its long hibernation in the basement storehouse of its temple, as

---

* This essay was originally published in *The Journal of Asian Studies*, 52 (1993), pp. 22-48.

an image worthy to travel abroad as an ambassador of independent India in the international diplomatics of traveling exhibitions.

All of us who attend to South Asian art realize that the "art objects" we admire so much in the Museum of Art or at the Festival of India are there, revealing themselves to us, as the result of a series of disjunctive historical events and processes. Certainly, we recognize that the nameless artists who produced these works were not working with museum display as their goal. Yet here, finally, they are.

Acts of appropriation, by which objects are removed from the settings for which they were fabricated and placed in new ones, are nothing new in South Asia. We would certainly be wrong to picture Islamic iconoclasm or European commoditization, however profound their impact, as impinging on a previously static Hindu, where all such objects occupied and remained in their own fixed places, recognized and respected by all. To the contrary, if we judge from inscriptions, chronicles, and the objects themselves, certain objects circulated widely and famously in early medieval India.

This essay will examine one phase in the circulation of Indian art objects: the appropriation of sculpted images by medieval Indian rulers as political acts. During this period, the worship of divinized images in temples was the central public religious cult of the subcontinent, and temple images were often closely tied to the political order. In the prevailing ideological formations of medieval India, worshipers of Vishnu, Śiva, or Durgā considered ruling authority to emanate from the lord of the cosmos downward to the human lords of more limited domains such as empires, kingdoms, territories, or villages. The construction of monumental temples housing images of these divinities, making evident their cosmic sovereignty within the polity of the sponsor, was a way of representing and embodying political accomplishments while locating such attainments within a larger, encompassing divine order.

With divine images already preponderant participants in the medieval system of authoritative relations, it is not surprising that images were often seized publicly by one ruler from another in circumstances of conflict. Alive to the identities and mythic backgrounds of the figures, royal looters dislodged selected images from their customary positions and employed them to articulate political claims in a rhetoric of objects whose principal themes were victory and defeat, autonomy and subjugation, dominance and subordination. Such acts were undertaken in deadly earnest and often had decisive effects for the human actors. For the images, too, there were notable consequences. Captured by new proprietors, relocated in new surroundings, their identities shifted significantly. Here I wish to explore this medieval political discourse that utilized religious images and its effect on the objects so used.

The Appropriation of Images

When art historians of religion, and others who concern themselves with Indian religious objects think about an image such as our hypothetical Dancing Śiva, we focus our attention most often on the aesthetic elegance of its form, on the religious meaning of its iconographic composition, or on the social and political context within which it was fabricated. In these matters, we believe, lies the essential significance of the object, the message the artist and other agencies responsible for its composition intended to convey. The subsequent life history of the object we tend to regard as extrinsic, as somehow beside the point. It is as if meaning were fixed once and for all at the moment of creation.

With these tacit assumptions, Indianists have seldom studied the appropriation of art objects in premodern South Asia. The only general treatment that I know of is *Royal Conquest and Cultural Migrations in South India and the Deccan* (1964), by the erudite art historian C. Sivaramamurti. In his wide-ranging survey of the relationship between military campaigns and the transmission of artistic themes and motifs in classical and medieval South Asia,

Sivaramamurti paints a portrait of essentially benign artistic exchanges among warring kings, motivated by spontaneous aesthetic appreciation.

> Sometimes a great victor was struck with admiration and adopted what were essential features of the culture of a dynasty long reduced to dust with all its glory forgotten. Sometimes the politically vanquished sovereign had something glorious to give as a lesson of culture to his victor, who, it must be said to his credit, enthusiastically accepted it, though it was really a cultural conquest of the political victor by the vanquished. (Sivaramamurti 1964b)

Undoubtedly, many medieval South Asian kings did appreciate the artistry of a finely rendered bronze or an elegant carved pillar, just as they appreciated well-created poetry. As prescriptive texts indicate, a young prince's education might well include instruction in the various branches of art and architecture. Kings often participated directly in the construction of religious edifices as ritual patrons, and several substantial texts on the fabrication of temples and images are attributed to royal authorship. However, kings did not regard the appropriation of an image as primarily an expression of aesthetic sensitivity, nor did they recognize the strong division of "political" and "cultural" domains implicit in Sivaramamurti's account. In almost all inscriptions and narrative accounts dealing with the matter, expropriations are treated as predominantly political acts. Such actions were not benign but were highly consequential, not only for the development of art, but for the subsequent course of political events as well.

To gain a preliminary idea of the value attached to image appropriations, let us consider the case of the pure-gold Buddha image of the Jewel Palace in Anurādhapura, seized by the Pāṇḍyans in the ninth century and regained by the Sinhalese king Sena II. The events are narrated by the Buddhist monk and chronicler Dhammakitti in the *Cūlavaṃsa* (*CV*) (Geiger 1925:115-36; 1929:138-60).†

† All translations from Pali, Sanskrit, and Tamil in this essay are mine. I also cite published translations where available.

In the early ninth century, the Pāṇḍyan kingdom of southern Tamilnad expanded northward into the Kaveri and Kongu regions, and sometime around 835 the Pāṇḍyan ruler Śrīmāra Śrīvallabha (r. 815-62), filled with imperial ambitions, mounted an invasion of the island of Sri Lanka. The Sinhala king Sena I (r. 831-51) attempted to resist, but the Pāṇḍyan attack proved too formidable.

> In an instant the great army of the Pāṇḍyan king swept over the large crowd of Sinhala soldiers and crushed them, moving like Māra's army. And the Sinhala king, hearing that his army had been sundered, took up all his portable wealth and fled the city, heading towards the mountains. (*CV* 50.19-20)

With the Sinhalese army dispersed and leaderless, Śrīmāra (like his namesake Māra, deadly to the Buddhists) easily captured the capital and began to plunder it.

> He removed all the valuables from the royal treasury, and seized everything that could be seized in the monastery and the city. The statue of the Teacher made entirely of gold in the Jewel Palace, the pair of jewels set as eyes in the Lord of Sages made of stone, likewise the gold plate on the *caitya* in the Thūpārāma, and the golden images in the various monasteries – all these he seized, denuding Lanka island of its wealth and spitting out the once-splendid city as if demons (yakṣas) had devoured it. (*CV* 50.33-36)

The solid gold Buddha was not an ancient image. It had been made about fifty years earlier, sponsored by King Mahinda II (r. 772-92) at the steep cost of 60,000 copper coins, and established on a pedestal in the Jewel Palace, a pavilion constructed by Mahinda in the Abhayagiri monastic complex (*CV* 48.136-37). Mahinda's grandson, Aggabodhi VIII (r. 801-12), honored the image with a grand festival as part of his accession to kingship (*CV* 49.44). The sumptuous image was evidently one of considerable importance not only to the Abhayagiri monks who maintained it but also to the Sinhalese rulers of the period.

Back on the mainland, the Pallavas were organizing a coalition of forces to oppose the upstart Pāṇḍyans, and this undoubtedly made Śrīmāra more eager to come to terms with his defeated opponent.

From exile, Sena I was able to negotiate a settlement with the occupying power, giving elephants and all his jewels to Śrīmāra. The Pāṇḍyan king left the island with his booty and tribute. Sena I returned to the capital and took up sovereignty once again, but sovereignty of a decidedly diminished stature.

When Sena I died, his nephew, Sena II (r. 851-85), became ruler. The new king ruled without incident, Dhammakitti relates, until the day he held a festival for the Tooth-relic:

> Once when the king was celebrating the great festival of the Tooth-relic with all proper offerings, he ascended the excellent Jewel Palace, and there saw the empty pedestal where the golden Buddha had once stood. "Why is this?" he asked.
>
> "Does the king not know?" replied the ministers. "During the time of your uncle, King Sena, my lord, the Pāṇḍyan king came here, laid waste to the island, and left, taking all that had become valuable to us."
>
> When the king heard this, he was ashamed as if it were he himself who had been defeated. And that very day he ordered the ministers to assemble his troops. (*CV* 51.22-26)

A disgruntled Pāṇḍyan prince, apparently a passed-over claimant to the throne, had conveniently appeared in Lanka requesting aid, and Sena II saw in him an opportunity to redress his grievance. The Sinhala king sent an expeditionary force to accompany the prince and support his claim to rule in Madurai, the Pāṇḍyan capital. "Go!" he ordered his commander, Kuṭṭaka, "Kill the Pāṇḍyan king! Bring back all the jewels he once took from here! Grant sovereignty to this prince, and return quickly!" (*CV* 51.30-31).

Meanwhile, the Pāṇḍyan armies had been engaged with the Pallava-led coalition, fighting three costly battles. When the Sinhalese armies attacked from the other flank and marched on Madurai, the Pāṇḍyans were unable to resist. Śrīmāra died shortly after of wounds sustained in battle.

> Then the Sinhalese armies fearlessly entered the city and plundered the place completely, like gods sacking the city of the demons. The

> commander inspected the treasury in the royal place, and took all the valuables that had been taken from our island, as well as those found in the town and the countryside. (*CV* 51.39-41).

A good patriot, Dhammakitti compares pillage done by others to the work of Māra's army and demons; when it is done by his own countrymen, however, it is as if gods plundered demons.

Kuṭṭaka had the Pāṇḍyan prince crowned as King Varaguṇavarman II and, after a brief tour, returned to Lanka, where Sena II received the victorious army with rejoicing and rituals of solidarity. The king held a great feast for them in the capital, celebrated a festival of victory, and distributed gifts to the poor. The repatriated objects he conscientiously restored to their proper places.

> Without attachment he placed all the valuables in their original places on the island, and he ritually established the golden images just as they had been before. He filled the empty pedestal of the Teacher in the Jewel Palace, and he secured the land by setting up guardposts. (*CV* 51.48-49)

The restoration of images had remarkable effects on the community, for from that time on Lanka became as prosperous as Uttarakuru, the legendary land of plenty beyond the Himālaya.

In this simple moral tale of treasure lost and recaptured, we begin to see more clearly how medieval kings and their advisers regarded the expropriation of images. The stolen image, disclosed to the young king by its empty pedestal, serves as an objectification of defeat not only for his uncle, who had suffered the loss, but for the very institution of Sinhala sovereignty. The humiliation that the king feels and his immediate resolve to retrieve the golden Buddha indicate how powerfully the empty pedestal provoked him, how clearly he understood its message in this discourse of objects. His orders to Kuṭṭaka and the commander's careful search in the royal treasury at Madurai confirm that recovery of the missing images was a central purpose of the invasion, and the jubilation upon their successful return is in the narrator's eyes a celebration of the restoration of the country's wholeness. For Dhammakitti, whose principal concern throughout the cūlavaṃśa is to delineate proper relations between Sinhalese sovereignty and the Buddhist community, loss and recovery of the golden Buddha is a synecdoche for the integrity of the Sinhalese polity itself.

Loot: Morality and Motivation

In their inscriptions, medieval Indian rulers proudly and repeatedly proclaim their expropriation of objects from other kings. Here, for instance, is the epigraphic account of a Cola king's victory over a Cālukya opponent at the battle of Kūṭalcaṅkamam:

> Vīrarājendra halted his hot, impetuous elephant and donned the garland of victory. He plucked out his opponent's wives, the family treasure, his conches, his fringed white parasol, his trumpets, his war-drum, his canopy, his white yak-tail fans, the banner of the boar, the crocodile gateway, "Blossom" the female elephant, a herd of war-elephants, and a troop of prancing horses. Amidst shouts of praise, he put on the victory crown adorned with splendid red jewels. (Hultzsch 1899a:34)

Not only does Vīrarājendra (1063-69) "pluck" his defeated enemy of these properties, he also places them on display in the capital for his subjects to view:

> Seated on a throne of bright jewels, Vīrarājendra exhibited in orderly rows the great heaps of treasures he had seized in the Vengi territory, while all the kings on earth did homage at his feet and praised him. (Hultzsch 1899b:67)

There is nothing furtive about all this. Just as the subordinate rulers bowing at Vīrarājendra's feet visibly signify their acceptance of his overlordship, the orderly exhibition of Cālukyan treasures is meant to represent objectively to all observers Vīrarājendra's battlefield victory. Looting in medieval South Asia, was an important element in the rhetoric of kingship.

The forcible expropriation of valued objects from an other defined as an enemy in circumstances of military conflict, which we designate by the Anglo-Indian term "looting," is a longstanding practice in many cultures, of course (Yule and Burnell 1903:519-

20). However, this activity may be constructed and construed differently in different times and places. We in the modern West have come to regard looting as a species of theft, a side effect of war that is predatory, disorganized, and motivated by economic gain.

Indians of the medieval period, by contrast, did not consider such seizure as theft, nor did they necessarily conduct it in a disorderly and surreptitious fashion. As the inscriptions of Vīrarājendra suggest, medieval South Asian rulers and their retinues carried out plunder as a normal and public aspect of war, organized by and around the person of the king, and directed as much toward symbolic objects as toward economic resources. To consider more closely the cultural construction of such wartime appropriations, let us begin with the *dharmaśāstra* of Manu (*MS*) and his ninth-century Kashmiri commentator Medhātithi (*MSBh*) (Jolly 1887; Buhler [1886] 1984; Kevalananda and Gharpure 1958; Jha 1920-26).

In his discussion of proper royal conduct, Manu is concerned to circumscribe battlefield behavior within a code of chivalrous conduct. Manu sets down prescriptions concerning whom a warrior may strike, when he may strike him, what weapons he may use, and much more. While urging discipline upon the troops in many respects, Manu indicates no similar compunction about the propriety of plunder.

> Chariots, horses, parasols, money, grain, cattle, women, all kinds of goods, and base metals all belong to the one who wins (*jayati*) them. (*MS* 7.96)

It is a matter of "victory," not of theft.

The moral question for Manu is not whether one may expropriate objects (and living property as well) from defeated opponents, but how one should properly distribute the booty. Certain valuable commodities, such as gold, silver, and land are reserved for the king alone, Medhātithi tells us. This includes, as we will see, all regalia and images. It is impermissible, however, for the king as master (*svāmin*) to appropriate all loot for himself. Other items – those listed in Manu's verse – belong to the individual warriors who acquire them. But here, too, a portion (and, Medhātithi specifies, the best portion) must be presented to the king: "One should give a share to the king. So it is stated in the Veda" (*MS* 7.97). The king occupies the center of all looting transactions. Sharing the spoils reiterates substantively the moral relationship between king and troops.

The Vedic precedent to which Manu refers is none other than the primordial battle between Indra, king of the gods, and the demon Vṛtra. When Indra defeated the demon in combat and so became great, he requested and received best portion of all the loot obtained (*Aitareyabrāhmaṇa* 3.21; Keith 1920:178). As Indra among the gods, so, too, the king among his subordinates is entitled to the choice part of every expropriation. By sharing loot hierarchically, Manu suggests, Hindu rulers should attempt to replicate in human society the model set by the Vedic gods.

Medhātithi records an additional provision concerning spoils gained by the king himself and those acquired by the army as a collectivity. Of such loot, he tells us, "the king should distribute it among those he supports according to the principle of 'bestowing acquisitions on a worthy recipient'" (*MSBh* 7.97). This principle, Medhātithi explains elsewhere, means that a king should apportion out his acquisitions to such "worthy recipients" as gods, hermitages, intellectuals, moral exemplars, and others of that ilk. He also may employ his resources in sponsoring public festivals (*MSBh* 7.56). By that same principle, we often learn through inscriptions of looted objects presented to temple deities and to those who served the king in battle. Booty engenders those substantive transactions that link the king both with the god or gods whose cosmic sovereignty includes and surpasses his own and also with eminent subjects within his own dominion.

Far from eschewing wartime appropriations, then, medieval Hindu rulers place themselves forthrightly in the center of a redistributive network involving expropriated objects. Not surprisingly, this is closely linked to the medieval Hindu ideology of royal authority, which views the king as the central agency responsible for integrating the dispersed segments of his domain into a unitary polity and bringing about its prosperity. By seizing objects during military campaigns, he embodies the victory he has attained over his rivals, symbolically incorporating their signs, and by reapportioning those objects within his own domain, he replenishes it and reiterates the ties that bind together the dominion of which he is the moral center.

Appropriated Images and Secondary Signs

The appropriation of Indian images recasts their significance without altering what they are and fundamentally represent. To clarify this point, it is useful to keep in mind Roland Barthes' well-known model of mythology as a second-order semiological system (1957:111-17). Here, the first-order sign system consists not of language but of physical objects – in most cases, sculpted objects that represent something according to known conventions and also may serve as the embodiment of that something. The golden Buddha image, as signifier, evokes immediately in its viewers the concept of "Buddha-as-Teacher," the signified. Their associative unity, drawn even more closely when the Buddha is ritually invoked into the image, constitutes the sign. It is this first-order pairing of image and signified concept (or divinity) that we refer to when we "identify" an Indian image iconographically. When seized by the Pāṇḍyan king, however, the signification of the golden Buddha shifts, as Barthes would have it, sideways. The appropriated image in its new situation now serves as the signifier also of the military victory of the Pāṇḍyan ruler over the Sinhalese. It has not lost its previous identity, but a secondary signification augments it.

This enhancement of identity may be asserted explicitly, as in the case of a Cālukyan door-guardian looted by the Cola king Rājādhirāja (r. 1018-54), where details of its origin and seizure have been inscribed onto the object itself: "This is the door-guardian brought by Lord Vijayarājendradeva after burning Kalyāṇapuram." The source of the looted image may become a permanent part of its name. The "Vātāpi Gaṇapati" at Tiruccenkāṭṭānkuṭi, for instance, denotes the image of Gaṇeśa brought to Tamilnad by the Pallava ruler Narasimhavarman I (r. 630-68), after sacking the Cālukyan capital of Vātāpi in 642 C.E. (Balasubrahmanyam 1975:96-102). Images may even carry with them entire pedigrees of previous proprietors and appropriators. In the Lakṣmaṇa temple of Khajurāho (illustration 1), constructed by the Candella ruler Yaśovarman shortly before 950 C.E. to house a solid-gold image of Viṣṇu Vaikuṇṭha, the foundation inscription traces the background of the image:

> The lord of the Tibetans got it from Mount Kailāśa, and then Sahi the king of Kangrā received it from him out of friendship. With his troops of elephants and horses, Herambapāla (Pratihāra) thereupon seized it from him. Obtaining it from his son, the (Pratihāra) prince Devapāla, the illustrious (Candella) king Yaśovarman – an ornament among kings and a crusher of enemies – performed the ritual establishment of Vaikuṇṭha. (Keilhorn 1892:129)

From "Kailāśa" (Kashmir?) to Tibet to Kangrā to Kanyakubja to Khajurāho: these past journeys of this eminent Viṣṇu image are carefully recorded as indicative and constitutive of its identity and value.

Appropriated images are, nevertheless, still also divine images. The object may be removed from its original and intended situation, but this does not empty it of its previous significance as a fabricated icon that may, under proper ritual conditions, serve as an embodiment for a god or goddess. Looted images are, therefore, worthy of respectful treatment from their new proprietors, and for the most part during this period they did receive it. We do not hear of the intentional defilement of divine images nor, very often, of their public mutilation by those who seize them.

Often the looters made considerable effort to erect new temples for housing plundered images in the manner that befitted

Illustration 1. Lakṣmaṇa Temple, Khajurāho, M.P. candella period, reign of Yaśovarman, 954 C.E. (Photograph courtesy American Institute of Indian Studies).

their significance. One of the most notable practitioners of royal appropriation was the Vijayanagar emperor Kṛṣṇadevarāya (r. 1509-29). Shortly after assuming the throne, the emperor attacked the forces of the Gajapati ruler Pratāparudra at Udayagiri, a hill stronghold in Andhra Pradesh. After a bitter siege lasting some eighteen months, the fortress fell, paving the way for further victories over the Gajapatis and leading finally to Prataparudra's acceptance of Vijayanagar suzerainty.

The victory at Udayagiri was celebrated as a momentous event, and as part of the celebrations Kṛṣṇadevarāya had transported back to his capital an image of Bālakṛṣṇa from a small temple at Udayagiri (Krishna Sastri 1912:164-200). It was a modest figure, just over three feet tall with its pedestal. Carved in the greenish black granite typical of the Udayagiri area, it portrayed Kṛṣṇa as a chubby boy seated with his right foot on a lotus flower and holding a butter-ball (illustration 2). To house the looted image, the emperor had specially constructed the Kṛṣṇasvāmi temple, resembling in plan and design the Udayagiri temple from which the image had been removed. At its consecration ceremony, the king presented gold and silver vessels to the Udayagiri Bālakṛṣṇa and endowed it with the royal share from nine villages for maintaining regular daily worship on a suitable scale (Krishna Sastri 1923:44-50). Vyasarāya, a favored intellectual of the royal court, composed a series of hymns to honor the advent of this image in Vijayanagar (Nilakanta Sastri and Venkataramanayya 1946:1.203). Evidently, Bālakṛṣṇa was treated as a valued and honored guest by his new dynastic hosts.

There is good reason to suppose that another Vijayanagar monument of Kṛṣṇadevarāya's time, the Viṭṭhalasvāmi temple, also housed a looted image. Viṭṭhala is a form of Viṣṇu-Kṛṣṇa worshipped almost exclusively in Maharashtra, and his cult is centered at Pandharpur. In 1520 and 1521, Kṛṣṇadevarāya led a successful campaign against 'Ādilshāh, Sultan of Bijapur, bringing him temporary control over the Pandharpur area. Considerable evidence suggests that the Vijayanagar ruler took the image of Viṭṭhala from its cult center and brought it back to the capital to animate his own Viṭṭhala temple, which was then under construction (Khare 1936).

For Kṛṣṇadevarāya, the appropriation of such images does not appear to have been simply a matter of personal religious predilection or of offering refuge from the threat of Islamic iconoclasm to gods of other regions (Longhurst 1916-17:27; Krishnasvami Aiyangar 1936:20-21). Rather, I would argue, it was part of a ritually incorporative imperial policy, requiring the conspicuous, ceremonial presence of subordinated polities in the capital. As Burton Stein has argued, during Navarātri, the principal royal festival of Vijayanagar, the feudatory "chiefs" were obliged to

Illustration 2. Bālakṛṣṇa, Udayagiri, A. P. Gajapati period, fifteenth century. Taken by Kṛṣṇadevarāya to Vijayanagar, 1514. Now in Government Museum, Madras. (Photograph courtesy Institut Français d' Indologie, Pondichery).

participate in a series of hierarchicized transactions with their overlord, enacting and reconstituting annually their subordinate share in Vijayanagar sovereignty (Stein 1983). Divinities of the subject regions likewise made yearly treks to attend the ceremonies, along with retinues of priests and temple dancers, who arrived in great "triumphal cars." While the human servants of these divinities made obeisance to the Vijayanagar emperor and danced for him, the images themselves expressed homage to the presiding deity of the festival, an image of the goddess Durgā, slayer of the Buffalo-demon.

The more permanent presence of the Udayagiri Bālakṛṣṇa in Vijayanagar conveyed much the same message as the visiting deities of Navarātri. Transported to the capital and housed in its own temple, it spoke, not only of the glorious childhood of Kṛṣṇa, who received the homage of Kṛṣṇadevarāya and his retinue, but also of the encompassing of Gajapati polity within the overarching imperial lordship of the Vijayanagar sovereign.

Homologies for Defeated Kings

Barthes' model of a second-order semiological system may also help account for the choice of particular objects or images as loot. The most common target for royal appropriation in medieval India, according to inscriptions, was regalia, a repertoire of objects closely associated with the king's person and his capacity to rule – banners, yak-tail fans, umbrellas, crowns, thrones, scepters, musical instruments, and gateways. With such synecdochic objects, the choice was rather simple. Since they were clearly and unequivocally associated with the king through an ongoing series of royal ceremonials, they presented obvious targets for seizure.

But divine images are more complex objects than other items of regalia, and similarly, the semiotic value of their appropriation was more complicated.

One might expect (as I initially did) that a conquering king would direct himself toward the most important images of a defeated kingdom. What more powerful way to proclaim dominance than to appropriate the preeminent deity of the vanquished. There are certainly cases where this expectation is borne out, such as the seizure of the Sinhalese Golden Buddha by the Pāṇḍyans. Not only was this image closely associated with Sinhalese royalty, but it also acted as an apt signifier for a polity that strongly supported the Buddhist Sangha as the primary religious group in its domain.

Just as often, however, this does not happen. Consider, for example, the perplexing choice of a stone door-guardian from Kalyāṇī as a target for appropriation by the Cola king Rājādhirāja.[‡] In 1045, Rājādhirāja waged war against his Cālukya foes led by Someśvara I (r. 1042-68), routed the enemy forces at the battle of Pūṇṭūr, forced Someśvara to flee, and then continued north to burn the Cālukya capital of Kalyāṇī. To add ritual insult to injury, he there performed a Heroic Consecration ceremony and assumed the new royal title of Vijayarājendra, the Victorious Rājendra. Returning from this successful campaign, Rājādhirāja transported a massive black stone door-guardian nearly 500 miles to his own capital of Gaṅgaikoṇḍacolapuram, where he displayed it as a trophy of war and had it incised with an identifying inscription stating that he had seized it when burning the Cālukya capital (Illustration 3).

Now, if Rājādhirāja plundered and burned Kalyāṇī, he presumably had his pick of a great number of Cālukya images. He could perhaps have taken an image of Viṣṇu in his Boar incarnation, which was the particular insignia of the Cālukya dynasty. To save Earth from sinking into the ocean, Viṣṇu had once embodied himself as a powerful Boar, dove into the depths, and raised Earth on his giant snout. The Cālukyas, emulating the earlier Gupta dynasty, adopted this form of Viṣṇu for special attention, seeking to re-enact the Boar's mythical deed through their own Earth-saving dynastic mission. Yet Rājādhirāja contented himself with an image of clearly inferior status within the temple hierarchy. Door-guardians were divine henchmen, stationed at the entrances of temples, whose business it was to prevent demons and enemies from approaching

‡ A more complete discussion of this case of appropriation, touching on many of the themes of this essay, may be found in Richard Davis, "Trophies of War: The Case of the Cālukya Intruder," in *Perceptions of India's Visual Past*, eds. Catherine Asher and Thomas Metcalf (Delhi: American Institute of Indian Studies, 1994).

the inner sanctum and to pay homage to the supreme lord within, thereby enacting and displaying their own subordinate position.

To comprehend Rājādhirāja's choice, it is first necessary to recognize that it alluded to a historical precedent, Dantidurga's famous "Golden Womb" (*hiraṇyagarbha*) ceremony at Ujjain. The first autonomous ruler of the Rāṣṭrakūṭa dynasty, Dantidurga (r. c. 742-56) gained independence from Lalitāditya of Kashmir and commenced a "conquest of the directions" (*digvijaya*), which brought him into conflict with the Gurjara-Pratihāra king, Nāgabhaṭa I, who ruled over the Malwa region. Dantidurga was victorious in the ensuing battle. He occupied the Gurjara capital, Ujjain, and there performed a royal gift-giving ceremony, the Golden Womb ritual. As one inscription relates it, "When he directed warriors to perform the Golden Womb ceremony in Ujjain, Dantidurga made the Gurjara ruler and other kings serve as his door-keepers (*Pratihāra*)" (Bhandarkar 1925-26:243). Clearly, the Rāṣṭrakūṭa king was here making a powerful ritual statement of political subjugation, forcing a defeated opponent to act in a lowly capacity in a royal Gift-giving ceremony, in his own capital to boot. Subsequently, Dantidurga went on to defeat the Cālukyas of Vātāpi (from whom the later Cālukyas of Kalyāṇī claimed descent), and the Rāṣṭrakūṭas replaced them for the next two centuries as the pre-eminent power of the Deccan.

The Cola kings of the eleventh century were acutely aware of the Rāṣṭrakūṭas. For one thing, the Rāṣṭrakūṭas had in the mid-tenth century dealt the Colas a humiliating defeat at the battle of Takkolam and had occupied Cola territory for several decades thereafter. More important, the Rāṣṭrakūṭas had been for almost two centuries the "supreme overlords" of the subcontinent, and the Cola kings Rājarāja I and Rājendra I – Rājādhirāja's grandfather and father, respectively – aspired to supersede them as the major imperial power of India. After two victorious "conquests of the directions," they had largely accomplished this. As a culmination of the Cola rise to pre-eminence, Rājendra mounted a grand northern progress to the Ganges River, which he had possessed and transported to

Illustration 3. Cālukya Door-guardian, Kalyāṇī, Karnataka. Later Cālukya period, tenth or early eleventh century. Taken by Rājādhirāja to Gaṅgaikoṇḍacolapuram, 1045. Now in Rājarāja Museum, Thanjavur. (Photograph courtesy American Institute of Indian Studies).

his own new capital – all of this replicating an earlier raid on the Ganges perpetrated by the Rāṣṭrakūṭas. (I will discuss the seizing of Gaṅgā below.)

So, too, Rājādhirāja looked to Rāṣṭrakūṭa precedents in his political rhetoric. His appropriation of a door-guardian from the later Cālukyas re-enacted Dantidurga's ritual demotion of the Gurjara king during the Golden Womb ceremony in a less personal and less compelling but more permanent manner. Mimicking the earlier conqueror of the Cālukyas, Rājādhirāja also performed a royal ritual in the capital of the defeated king – in this case, Heroic Consecration. Unable to force his rival to take on the role of ceremonial doorkeeper in person, since Someśvara had successfully fled, Rājādhirāja seized a stone door-guardian instead and transported it back to the Cola country.

The parallelism of door-guardian and Cālukya king went further still: both had failed in their primary responsibility. The hapless door-guardian had been unable to stop the destruction of its temple, and likewise Someśvara had failed to prevent the Cola armies from entering and destroying his capital. Waiting in attendance at the Cola capital, the looted Cālukya door-guardian could act as a permanent visible homologue of the subjugated Cālukya ruler. It was a taunting display, to be sure, and, not surprisingly, Someśvara returned from exile to avenge his humiliation by killing Rājādhirāja at the battle of Koppam.

Redistribution: The Emerald Pedestal

Not only does the seizing of objects from opponents in war convey political messages, so, too, does the subsequent redistributing of those objects. If an image forcibly taken from an unwilling opponent and repositioned in one's capital can serve as a figurative incorporation of that opponent's polity, then by the same token an image accepted willingly by a subordinate ruler from his overlord may signify a subjugation voluntarily accepted. The operative principle in such cases is Manu's phrase, "bestowing acquisitions on worthy recipients."

Within the system of loot-distribution described by Manu and Medhātithi, as we have seen, all important appropriated objects reverted to the king, who then "bestowed" them as warranted. The "worthy recipient" that he chose to favor might be, first and foremost, the god he worshiped as his own lord. So when the Kalacuri king Lakṣmaṇarāja II, ruling in the Dāhala region of Madhya Pradesh, undertook in the tenth century a western military campaign, he pointedly made a pilgrimage to the famous Śaiva temple of Somanātha on the Gujarat coast and there "presented in reverence to Śiva an image Kāliya [presumably Kāliyavadha Kṛṣṇa] made of jewels and gold," which he had taken in an earlier battle with the king of Orissa on the coast (Mirashi 1995:213-14).

Alternatively, a king might choose human subordinates as worthy recipients for looted images, not as an act of devotion to a superior but as one favor or grace to an inferior. To consider the political semantics of such a gift, let us take the case of an "Emerald Pedestal" (*marakatapītām*) employed as a central ritual object in an impressive performance of Navarātri in Ramanathapuram in the year 1892 (Sivasankara Pandiyaji n.d.; Breckenridge 1977). The pedestal was a looted object. According to local tradition, it had been acquired in the mid-seventeenth century by the Setupati Raghunātha Tevar, an ancestor of H.H. Raja Bhaskaraswamy Avargal, the Setupati sponsoring the 1892 celebrations.

At the time of its acquisition, the Madurai Nāyakkar ("governor") Tirumalai (r. 1623-59) was ruling over southern Tamilnad, virtually autonomous from the fading Vijayanagar imperium that had established the Nāyakkar rule in Madurai a century earlier. Raghunātha Tevar, the Setupati of Ramnad, was his subordinate. During Tirumalai's reign, the southern kingdoms of Madurai and Mysore had fought a series of inconclusive battles, and in 1656, with the aged Tirumalai sick in bed, the Mysore ruler Kaṇṭhīrava Narasa attacked once again. Apparently, the Mysore forces penetrated all the way to Madurai, and Tirumalai's only recourse was to call on his royal subordinate. The Madurai chronicles narrate it this way:

> Now the king Tirumalai Nāyakkar wrote and sent a letter to the Setupati. On the very day the Setupati read the letter, he immediately prepared 60,000 men and brought them. He defeated the Mysore army, drove it into the Ghats, attained victory, and returned to the king.
>
> The king was very happy, and held a feast for him in the palace. He presented him with many elephants and horses, clothing, ornaments, and the like, and he gave him the title "Tirumalai's Setupati." He also gave the Setupati his own Lion faced Palanquin and other emblems such as a banner and a canopy. Calling him a son of his own lineage, Tirumalai dismissed all revenue assessments, saying that he no longer had to pay tribute. And from that time on, the Setupati ruled his territory without paying tribute, and he had the Ramanathapuram fort rebuilt as a stone fortress. (Taylor 1853:2.26)

The transactions between the Ramnad Setupati and the Madurai Nāyakkar described here reflect a characteristic medieval South Indian patterning of authoritative relations by which ruling kings "shared" their sovereignty with lesser kings, who thereby became subordinate participants within the overarching system. In his recent ethnohistory of this political formation, Nicholas Dirks (1987) points to the Vijayanagar ceremony of Navarātri as the dramatic ritual paradigm of the system in action. During the nine-day ceremony, the Vijayanagar emperor at the center of the festival expressed his homage to an image of the goddess Durgā, the presiding deity of the festival, and received from her his authority to rule in the objective form of royal sword and scepter. In her defining mythic action, Durgā had herself received weapons from all the gods to aid her in killing the demon that none but she could defeat. The subordinate governors, Nāyakkars, who where compelled to be present in the capital, would in turn express their devotion to the emperor and receive from him portions of his authority in the physical form of emblems.

> The sharing of the king's sovereignty through the transactions of the festival had the effect of incorporating the disparate elements of

> the kingdom into his sovereign being and rendering them all parts – metonyms – of himself, even as the emblems were themselves metonyms of his sovereignty. (Dirks 1987:42)

This personalized and embodied authority was passed down from level to level, from emperor to governor to subordinate chieftain and so on, through similar ceremonial exchanges.

The primary currency of this hierarchized transactional system, Dirks tells us, were "services" and "honors": the subordinate offering service to his superior, the superior in turn granting honors of various sorts to the subordinate. So the Ramnad Setupati unhesitatingly offered his military service and troops to the beleaguered Madurai Nāyakkar, saving Tirumalai from defeat and attaining victory over the Mysore invaders on behalf of his overlord. The Emerald Pedestal presumably was part of the substantive "victory" that Raghunātha acquired during the campaign and presented to his lord. Tirumalai in turn recognized Raghunātha's service with a host of honors: gifts, titles, emblems, and rights to the unfettered enjoyment of land. These royal gifts were, in fact, gifts also of limited, shared sovereignty within Tirumalai's encompassing dominion.

In this light, it is not difficult to see why Tirumalai chose the looted pedestal as a suitable object to bestow upon his worthy recipient. During an earlier campaign on behalf of the Madurai ruler, Raghunātha had helped a Muslim invasion led by "Khub Khan" and had been honored with the title, "He who propped up the kingdom" (Nelson 1868:3.138). As a subordinate ruler and warrior, the Setupati certainly had acted as a prop to the Nāyakkar's rule, and so the identity of the plundered object once again refers to a political relationship. The Emerald Pedestal was a homologue not for an involuntarily subjugated source but for a willingly subordinate recipient.

The Gift of Submission

In one final variation on this general trope, an image might be given as a token of submission, a metonymic acceptance of ritual subordination, to forestall an actual invasion and a more forcible incorporation. Our example here concerns the Rāṣṭrakūṭas and Sinhalese.

In the early part of the ninth century, the Rāṣṭrakūṭa king Govinda III (r. c. 790-815) undertook two southern expeditions, during which he decisively defeated the most potent southern kingdom, the Pallavas of Kāñcīpuram, and occupied their capital. Other kingdoms of the south came under direct threat from this most powerful Indian empire, and the frightened Sri Lankan king Aggabodhi VIII, ruling in Anurādhapuram, did what he could to fend off a direct attack: he sent two images to Govinda. As a Rāṣṭrakūṭa inscription reports:

> Just as if he had forcibly subdued the self-centered [Lankan] king and his indolent chief minister with his own scepter and brought them deaf and dumb to the City of Delight, while in Kāñcī Govinda received from Lanka two images of their lord (*prabhu*) and then set them up in a Śaiva temple here [in Mānyakheṭa, the Rāṣṭrakūṭa capital], like two pillars of his fame. (Bhandarkar 1925-26:246)

The epigraphical simile makes it clear that these images were to be regarded as "deaf and dumb" representatives of a Sinhala polity that had, by this very gift, accepted the overlordship of the Rāṣṭrakūṭas. For Govinda III, more concerned with pillars of fame and ritual hegemony than the acquisition of territory, this was sufficient. The enforced diplomatic offering of images did dissuade the Rāṣṭrakūṭas from invading the island, but only at the expense of incorporating Lanka metonymically into the Rāṣṭrakūṭa imperial formation.

What exactly were the images that the Sinhalese king sent to Govinda? Various possibilities have been suggested: statues of the demon Rāvaṇa as "the most ancient and traditional ruler" of Lanka, or perhaps likenesses of the king and chief minister themselves (Bhandarkar 1925-26:241; Altekar 1934:69). In light of the general rhetoric we have investigated in this paper, it seems much more likely that Aggabodhi sent two images of the Buddha, as his own personal lord and the highest lord of the Sinhala polity. (Aggabodhi, we may recall, celebrated his royal consecration by honoring the solid-gold Buddha of the Jewel Pavilion.) It is possible, too, that the similitude of image and ruler had been drawn even more closely by casting the Buddha image according to the proportions of the king, a Sinhala practice of "reign-images" that has been documented for the tenth century if not earlier (Wickremasinghe 1912:213-29; Gunawardana 1979:175). Even without this close visual resemblance, though, none of the agents involved would have misread the clear statement of Sinhala subordination in the two Buddha images displayed "like pillars of fame" in a Śaiva temple of the Rāṣṭrakūṭa capital.

Imperial Sovereignty: The Capture of Rivers

The appropriations and relocations of the art objects considered so far speak primarily of personalized relations of dominance and subordination among rulers and of the incorporation of particular kingdoms into other polities. But other targets of appropriation make more far-reaching assertions.[§] Consider the inscriptional claims of Vinayāditya, ruler of the Cālukyas of Vātāpi in the late seventh century.

The Cālukyas at this time were the dominant power of the Deccan and had battled repeatedly with the Pallavas of Kāñcī for control of southern India. Taking advantage of a period of dynastic confusion in North India following the death of Harṣa in 647, Vinayāditya and his son, the crown prince Vijayāditya, undertook a northern campaign in about 690, where they were successful against a series of unnamed foes. They returned to the Deccan with great spoils, including a series of significant symbolic objects: the *pālī*-banner, the *ḍaḍhakka* drum, the "great sounds" (*mahāśabda*, probably conches), and the two rivers, "Gaṅgā and Yamunā." Gaining these, inscriptions tell us, Vinayāditya possessed

§ The recent work of Ronald Inden is particularly pertinent to this section. See, especially, his discussion of the Rāṣṭrakūṭa imperial formation (Inden 1990:228-62).

"all the insignia (*cihna*) of highest overlordship (*paramaiśvarya*), beginning with the powerful *pālī*-banner, which he had acquired by defeating all the lords of the northern regions" (Pathak 1907-8:202). They were passed on to Vijayāditya (r. 696-733) when he assumed the Cālukya throne, and he also came to possess "sovereignty illuminated by insignia such as the *pālī*-banner that cause the manifestation of complete overlordship" (Pathak 1909-10:16). The Cālukya inscriptions portray this particular bundle of loot not merely as the regalia or second-order signifier of a single enemy ruler but as the embodiment or representation of "universal sovereignty," imperial lordship of the highest order.

Evidently, we have here some extraordinary imperial objects. The *pālī*-banner (or, literally, "flags in rows"), singled out in Cālukya inscriptions as the insignia par excellence, seems to have been a particular arrangement of banners, in which a central flagstaff with the Cālukya insignia, Viṣṇu's Boar incarnation, on top was surrounded by rows of flags bearing insignia of all other dynasties in lower and peripheral position (Chidanandamurthy 1973:85-88). It was thus, as Ronald Inden points out, an indexical sign of the Cālukya's claim to the highest degree of sovereignty, encompassing and surpassing all other rulers of India (Inden 1990:250-52).

The most curious and intriguing items in this set of transportable objects, however, are the two rivers, Gaṅgā and Yamunā. The Gaṅgā may shift course gradually over the years, but how could the Cālukya king, ruling some 800 miles to the south of the river, claim to "take" Gaṅgā? What exactly did he appropriate? Gaṅgā and Yamunā are not just rivers but also goddesses whose images often adorn the entrances of North India temples. Is that perhaps what Vinayāditya seized?

The Cālukyas, it turns out, were not the only southerners to obtain Gaṅgā and Yamunā. Within sixty years of Vinayāditya's northern expedition, the Rāṣṭrakūṭas had supplanted the Cālukyas as the dominant power of the Deccan and acquired the authoritative *pālī*-banner, replacing the Cālukyan Boar on top with their own insignia, Viṣṇu's mount, Garuḍa. Around 800, the Rāṣṭrakūṭa king Govinda III also made an expedition into North India, directed against the Gurjara and Pāla kings, who were then battling for control of the Doab and the imperial city of Kanyakubja. He defeated the Gurjara king Nāgabhaṭa II, then marched farther north, where the Pāla king Dharmapāla and his Kanyakubja protégé, Cakrāyudha, also deferred to the royal Rāṣṭrakūṭa progress. During this campaign, the inscriptions say, Govinda "took from his enemies the Gaṅgā and Yamunā, made beautiful by their waves, and acquired at the same moment that supreme lordship of which they are a visible sign" (Fleet 1883:156-65). Once again, acquisition of the two northern rivers was epigraphically linked with the attainment of imperial sovereignty.

Two hundred years after that, when the Rāṣṭrakūṭas were no more and the Colas were the dominant power of peninsular India, the Cola emperor Rājendra I sent an army from Tamilnad north to capture the Ganges. Though well aware of the historical precedents for such an expedition, Rājendra instead chose to have himself compared with the mythical ascetic who also had altered the course of the Ganges.

> Mocking the great sage Bhagīratha, who had brought the Gaṅgā to earth through the power of his austerities, this light of the Solar lineage decided to purify his own domain with the Gaṅgā waters, brought there by the strength of his arms. (Krishna Sastri 1920:400)

The Cola army made its way north, engaging and defeating a variety of opponents until they finally reached the banks of the holy river. From there, golden pots of Gaṅgā water were transported south, according to inscriptional accounts, carried atop the heads of kings defeated along the way (Krishna Sastri 1984:74).

A pattern is clear. Three major peninsular dynasties of the early medieval period, each in its time the most powerful kingdom in the subcontinent, mounted military forays into the Gangetic plain, won skirmishes with whatever powers they encountered there, and claimed to have brought back to their own domains Gaṅgā and Yamunā in some sort of visible, substantive form. Moreover, none of them made any attempt in these raids to capture or retain territory in the Gangetic plain. Rāṣṭrakūṭa accounts admit this quite explicitly.

> In battles Govinda seized the noble, unshakable fame of the kings Nāgabhaṭa and Candragupta, and then – holding the acquisition of fame as his highest aim – he plucked out the remaining kings, now deprived of support, from their own lands as if he were picking grains of rice, and reinstated them again in their very own places. (Bhandarkar 1925-26:245)

The seemingly unacquisitive character of the expeditions perplexed earlier dynastic historians, who generally dismissed them as inconsequential, quixotic, and purposeless. The rulers themselves clearly did not regard their campaigns as inconsequential, however, for they repeatedly proclaimed them in inscriptions. First of all, the "plucking and replanting" maneuver incorporated the subjugated opponents into the imperial system, even while leaving them in place. Further, the raids were concerned predominantly with, in Rāṣṭrakūṭa terms, the "acquisition of fame" – and fame that could be objectified in the capture of particular symbolic objects. The peninsular powers regarded these objects as necessary to "manifest" or "make visible" their claims to supreme sovereignty. In medieval India, appropriating these signs of imperial sovereignty was a crucial part of constructing what Ronald Inden calls an "imperial formation."

An imperial formation in medieval India, as Inden describes it, was not a single state under centralized administrative control, nor was it a congeries of petty states warring against one another. Rather, it was a single complex polity ruled by a king of kings who exercised his sovereignty, directly or ritually, over other would-be claimants throughout the subcontinent (Inden 1990:29-33, 213-17). In the "scale of kingships" (or "circle of kings," as Indian treatises on statecraft put it), other kings would be compelled to recognize the imperial sovereign as pre-eminent, for instance, by rendering ceremonial homage at his court or through the forced attendance of an iconic stand-in at the imperial capital. They became, willingly or not, subordinate sharers in the transcending sovereignty of the king of kings who managed to create or maintain an imperial formation. Of course, subordinated rulers could always contest the ruling hegemony by claiming autonomy and seeking to construct their own "circle," but always with the risk that the empire might strike back. Given the considerable strategic problems in holding together such a polity, only a few dynasties succeeded in constituting longstanding imperial formations in medieval India, and the Rāṣṭrakūṭas of the eighth through tenth centuries and the Colas of the eleventh and twelfth centuries were the most formidable exemplars.

What did the rivers Gaṅgā and Yamunā have to do with all this? Prior to the time of the Cālukya ruler Vinayāditya, every major imperial kingdom of India had been centered on the Gaṅgā-Yamunā river system. The Magadha and Maurya empires had ruled from Pāṭaliputra, and the imperial Kuṣāṇas had maintained a capital at Mathura. The Guptas originated at Prayāga, the very confluence of Gaṅgā and Yamunā, and ruled from there or Pāṭaliputra. From the time of Candragupta II, imperial Guptas prominently featured statuary of Gaṅgā and Yamunā in shrines throughout their domain, evoking their own political center even as they invoked the presence of the two goddesses (Goyal 1967; Williams 1982:45-46). Later, Harṣa moved his capital from the relatively peripheral Sthāneśvara, along the upper reaches of the Yamunā, to the more central Kanyakubja when he attained imperial status.

Faced with this political Gangocentricity, a regional power aspiring to more encompassing imperial sovereignty had a choice of moving to the center, as Harṣa did, or of attempting to relocate the center at one's own capital. The Cālukyas, Rāṣṭrakūṭas, and Colas evidently chose the second option. In their own version of Muhammad-and-the-mountain, they brought not only the mountain – in the form of the Mount Kailāśa-style temples of Śiva that they each constructed – but also the river that issued from that mountain to their own sovereign selves, remaking in the process the imperial topography of the subcontinent (Inden 1990:256-62).

In what form did they effect this? In the case of the Colas, inscriptions state explicitly that Rājendra had Gaṅgā water transported in pots. With the Cālukyas and Rāṣṭrakūṭas, the evidence is not so clear. Gaṅgā and Yamunā are simply mentioned in lists of insignia, along with other items of regalia such as banners and musical instruments, indicating only that they are material things of some sort. A Rāṣṭrakūṭa inscription does tell us that Gaṅgā and Yamunā are "made beautiful by their waves," which describes the rivers themselves, of course, but would also apply to banners waving in the breeze or to graceful sculpted images. Scholars have offered at least three hypotheses: the Cālukyas and Rāṣṭrakūṭas

Illustration 4. Lād Khān temple, Aihole, Karnataka. Early Western Cālukya period, late seventh or early eighth century. (Photograph courtesy American Institute of Indian Studies).

seized images of the goddesses Gaṅgā and Yamunā; they seized banners with Gaṅgā and Yamunā imprinted on them; or they took pots containing water from the two rivers. All are plausible. In light of the recurrent plundering of images to make political statements during the medieval period, however, I considered it most likely that the Deccan powers looted images of Gaṅgā and Yamunā from existing temples at Prāyaga or Kanyakubja.

Even if they were not themselves images, though, the appropriation of Gaṅgā and Yamunā had an important bearing on the art of their new homes. Both Cālukyas and Rāṣṭrakūṭas appear to have commemorated their acquisitions by constructing shrines with Gaṅgā and Yamunā prominently featured. At Lād Khān temple in Aihole, probably built during the reign of the Cālukya king Vijayāditya, images of the two river-goddesses are located on the outer columns of the porch, displayed like trophies (Illustration 4). Further, Gaṅgā and Yamunā appear as important icons in Cālukyan art only from this time on. It is not a matter of a slowly permeating northern iconographic figure finally reaching the Deccan. Rather, it appears that the Cālukyas only now felt that they had attained the degree of sovereignty where they could display with confidence (and without fear of retribution) the North Indian river-goddesses. As for the Rāṣṭrakūṭas, Govinda III was probably responsible for construction of the shrine of the Three River-Goddesses at Ellora, and adjunct to the great Kailāśa rock-cut temple built there by his predecessor Kṛṣṇa I (Goetz 1974:91-107). Three large panels on the rear wall depict Gaṅgā at the center flanked by Yamunā and Sarasvatī, the subtle river that joins the other two at Prāyaga. After the Rāṣṭrakūṭa exploits in the Doab, the Rāṣṭrakūṭas began to include Gaṅgā and Yamunā on their imperial seals, just as the Cālukyas had.

The most dramatic commemoration of Gaṅgā-capture, however, was that of Rājendra. When the waters reached the Cola territories, Rājendra had a "liquid pillar of victory" made of Gaṅgā-water, designated the "Cola-Gaṅgā," constructed in the new capital that he had just built, Gaṅgaikoṇḍacolapuram, the "city of the Cola king who took the Gaṅgā." Presiding over the city was a new Kailāśa-like imperial Śiva temple (Illustration 5). Rājendra furnished the city and the temple with objects and images seized in the course of his conquests: from the Cālukyas a Sun-pedestal, several images of Durgā, and a Gaṇeśa image; from the eastern Cālukyas, a resting Nandi, Śiva's bull mount; from the Kaliṅgas

Illustration 5. Bṛhadīśvara temple, Gaṅgaikoṇḍacolapuram, Tamilnad. Cola period, reign of Rājendra I, c. 1030.

of Orissa, three large stone images of Bhairava and Bhairavī and an awesome eight-armed Kālī image; from the Pālas of Bengal, a

in extreme situations. Take, for instance, the muddled image raid of the Gauḍa soldiers, described by Kalhaṇa in his *Rājataraṅgiṇī* (*RT*) (Stein 1892:56; Sitaram Pandit 1935:125-26).

The great eighth-century Kashmiri ruler Lalitāditya, according to Kalhaṇa's reckoning, was for the most part a high-minded monarch, but he was also capable of duplicity in the service of imperial policy. Once, after making a promise of safe conduct to the king of Gauḍa (Bengal) and offering as surety (*madhyastha*; literally, "intermediary") the image of Viṣṇu Parihāsakeśava, Lalitāditya treacherously ordered the king assassinated. Such a brazen act clearly departed from all standards of proper royal conduct and called for revenge. As we might expect, the reprisal was directed not at the perpetrator of the deed but at its intermediary. A troop of the murdered king's dedicated attendants sneaked into Kashmir posing as pilgrims and made their way toward the temple of Parihāsakeśava.

Now Parihāsakeśava was not just any image. After Lalitāditya's successful conquest of the directions in the mid-eighth century, making him the premier ruler of North India, he returned to Kashmir and established a new capital at the confluence of the Vitastā and Sindhu rivers, Parihāsapura. In and around the new capital, Lalitāditya and his retinue established a number of shrines, but the dominant one was a *sarvatobhadra* temple dedicated to Viṣṇu Parihāsakeśava (Inden 1985). A *sarvatobhadra* temple was the highest form of temple structure, and the immense, silver Parihāsakeśava that stood at its center was an image of Viṣṇu Vaikuṇṭha, the cosmic overlord whose four visages, facing in the cardinal directions, represented Viṣṇu's four primary emanations. This was the principal ruling image of the empire that Lalitāditya had established, and to attack it was to threaten the very center of that polity.

Outside the temple, the Gauḍa soldiers mustered, preparing to destroy the imperial image. Fortunately for Lalitāditya, however, the priests of Parihāsakeśava were a vigilant lot, and the Gauḍa

Illustration 6. Durgā Mahiṣāsuramardinī, Karnataka. Later Cālukya period. Early eleventh century. Now in Gaṅgaikoṇḍacolapuram. (Photograph courtesy Institut Français d'Indologie, Pondichery).

image raiders were not well-acquainted with the fine points of Kashmiri images.

> Though the king was abroad, the priests observed that the soldiers wanted to enter, and they closed the gates of the Parihāsakeśava shrine. Aroused with boldness, the soldiers got ahold of the silver Ramasvāmin image, which they mistook for Parihāsakeśava. They carried it out and ground it into dust. And even as Lalitāditya's troops who had come out from the city were killing them at each step, the Gauḍas continued to break it into particles and scatter them in every direction. (*RT* 4.326-28)

The image of Ramasvāmin, silver as was Parihāsakeśava, had been excavated some years earlier by Lalitāditya in a remote part of Kashmir (*RT* 4.265-76). The king had it brought to the capital, and a small stone shrine was built for it near the Parihāsakeśava temple. Although supposed to be an ancient image (Lalitāditya claimed it had been established by Rāma himself), it certainly did not possess the imperial grandeur of Parihāsakeśava. As clearly indicated by the shrine housing it, Rāmasvāmin occupied a position subordinate to the imperial image of Viṣṇu within the hierarchy of Kashmiri divinities.

By this token, then, the image raid of the Gauḍa avengers was a botched affair. They failed to destroy Lalitāditya's central ruling image, the image that had stood as deceitful assurance of their own king's security, and they mistakenly crushed a lesser icon. But this is not the moral that Kalhaṇa draws from the incident. Rather, he chooses to praise the extraordinary devotion that the raiders showed to their former lord.

> The showers of their blood illuminated their uncommon devotion (*bhakti*) to their lord, and the earth itself was enriched. . . . What a lengthy path they traveled! And what devotion they showed to their deceased ruler! The Creator himself could not accomplish what the Gauḍa soldiers achieved that day. (*RT* 4.330-32)

Utter devotional commitment to a lord (whether divine or human) may in certain circumstances transcend normal moral evaluation. Where the provocation is great, devotion may transmute normally immoral acts into exemplary ones. The Gauḍa raiders, however, were not the only ones to demonstrate loyalty to their superior.

> When those Gauḍa demons (*rākṣasa*) brought destruction, the holy Parihāsakeśava, the king's favored image, was protected through the sacrifice of Rāmasvāmin. (*RT* 4.334)

Images, too, are capable of bhakti toward their lords.

Final Destinations

The story did not necessarily end there for these images. Many of the objects referred to in this article did suffer subsequent destruction. The solid-gold Buddha of the Abhayagiri monastery, for example, undoubtedly was destroyed in the 1017 Cola raid carried out by Rājendra on Anurādhapura.

> They broke into the relic chambers in the three chambers and throughout Lanka, stealing many costly images of gold and other metals. They violently destroyed all the monasteries everywhere, and like yakṣas sucking blood they took away all the treasures of Lanka. (*CV* 55.20-21)

The two Buddhas sent by Aggabodhi VIII to appease the Rāṣṭrakūṭa threat were destroyed either in the 972 razing of Mānyakheṭa by the Paramāra ruler Harṣasīyaka or in the 1007 sack by Rājendra Cola. The bejeweled Kāliyavadha Kṛṣṇa image that Lakṣmaṇaraja Kalachuri stole from Orissa and gave to the deity at Somanātha was no doubt expropriated during Maḥmūd's 1026 destruction of the temple and, following Ghaznavid policy, it would have been melted down along with other metal idols to gild the mosque at Ghazna.

Several of the images, though, have escaped such fates and have been able to continue their lives resituated as art objects in Indian museums. Thus, the small stone Bālakṛṣṇa carried by Kṛṣṇadevarāya from Udayagiri to his own capital in 1512 was thrown from its pedestal and its arms broken, perhaps in 1565, when Muslim armies overran the city. Such desecration and mutilation would have excluded the object from further ritual use. For art objects, however, a degree of mutilation is not necessarily a debit, for it may serve to certify age and authenticity. So, when the archaeologist A. H. Longhurst found the image lying among the debris of its disused temple in the early twentieth century, he sent it off to join the collection of the Government Museum in Madras.

Museums are contexts too, of course, and the Udayagiri Bālakṛṣṇa once again has taken on a new significance in its new location as part of a Museological narrative of national identity. As we have seen, the appropriated Child-Kṛṣṇa image had been previously set up in its temple at Vijayanagar both to be worshiped as an icon of the god Kṛṣṇa and to serve as a synecdoche for the Gajapati kingdom subsumed within the encompassing Vijayanagar imperial formation. But the political formations and agonistic relations within which such rhetorical claims were stated and made sense were themselves transient, and, when Gajapati and Vijayanagar existed no more as polities, the metonymic role of the Udayagiri Bālakṛṣṇa would no longer have any currency.

Its new role derives rather, from the colonial and postcolonial project of constructing an Indian national identity, a project in which past antagonisms are effaced whenever possible in pursuit of a more encompassing unity. This unity most often has been considered to lie in the cultural domain rather than in any past political formation, for, as the Government Museum's centennial souvenir volume put it, "in spite of its great diversity, Indian culture has a common basic pattern." During the twentieth century, religious objects and artifacts of all sorts, embodying the collective artistic heritage of the Indian nation, have been collected, dated, organized, and exhibited in the Madras Museum. Since 1939, the sculptural arts of India have been arranged chronologically, grouped according to major imperial periods, to present to the Indian public an account of its own artistic history in images. Here the Udayagiri Bālakṛṣṇa that once signified Gajapati subordination takes its place as a representative of the "Vijayanagar period (1300-1600)."

For it, as for many Indian objects, the medieval rhetoric of objects, of victory and incorporation, has given way to the museological rhetoric of historical sequence and cumulative cultural heritage.

References

Altekar, A.S. 1934. *The Rashtrakutas and Their Times*. Poona Oriental Series. Poona: Oriental Book Agency.

Balasubrahmanyam, S.R. 1975. *Middle Chola Temples: Rājarāja I to Kulottunga I (A. D. 985-1070)*. Faridabad: Thomson Press.

Barthes, Roland. 1957. *Mythologies*. New York: Hill and Wang.

Bhandarkar, D.R. 1925-26. "Sanjan Plates of Amoghavarsha I." *Epigraphia Indica* 18:235-57.

Breckenridge, Carol Appadurai. 1977. "From Protector to Litigant – Changing Relations Between Hindu Temples and the Raja of Ramnad." *Indian Economic and Social History Review* 14:75-106.

Buhler, Georg, trans. [1886] 1984. *The Laws of Manu*. Sacred Books of the East, vol. 25. Delhi: Motilal Banarsidass.

Chidanandamurthy, M. 1973. "The Meaning of 'Pālīdhvaja': A Reinterpretation." In *Srikanthika Sastri Felicitation Volume*. Mysore: Geetha Book House.

Cohn, Bernard. 1985. "The Transformation of Objects into Artefacts, Antiquities and Art in 19th Century India." Unpublished paper presented at National Endowment for the Humanities Conference, "Patronage in Indian Culture."

Davis, Richard H. 1994. "Trophies of War: The Case of the Cālukya Intruder." In Catherine Asher and Thomas Metcalf, eds., *Perceptions of India's Visual Past*. Delhi: American Institute of Indian Studies.

Dirks, Nicholas B. 1987. *The Hollow Crown: Ethnohistory of an Indian Kingdom*. Cambridge: Cambridge University Press.

Fleet, J. F. 1883. "Sanskrit and Old Canarese Inscriptions, No. 127." *Indian Antiquary* 12:156-65.

Geiger, Wilhelm, ed. 1925. *Cūlavaṃsa: Being the More Recent Part of the Mahāvaṃśa*. Pali Text Society Text Series, No. 20. London: Humphrey Milford.

________ Trans. 1929. *Cūlavaṃsa: Being the More Recent Part of the Mahāvaṃśa*. Pali Text Society Translation Series, No. 18. London: Oxford University Press.

Goetz, Hermann. 1974. "The Kailāśa of Ellora and the Chronology of Rāṣṭrakūṭa Art." In *Studies in the History, Religion and Art of Classical and Medieval India*. Wiesbaden: Franz Steiner Verlag.

Goyal, Shriram. 1967. *A History of the Imperial Guptas*. Allahabad: Central Book Depot.

Gunawardana, R. A. L. H. 1979. *Robe and Plough: Monasticism and Economic Interest in Early Medieval Sri Lanka*. Association for Asian Studies: Monographs and Papers. Tucson: University of Arizona Press.

Hultzsch, E. 1899a. "Inscriptions in the Pasupatisvara Temple at Karuvur." *South Indian Inscriptions* 3:31-39.

_______1899b. "Inscriptions at Manimangalam." *South Indian Inscriptions* 3:64-71.

Inden, Ronald. 1985. "The Temple and the Hindu Great Chain of Being." *Puruṣārtha* 8.

_______1990. *Imagining India*. Oxford: Basil Blackwell.

Jha, Ganganatha, trans. 1920-26. *Manusmṛti: The Laws of Manu with the Bhāṣya of Medhātithi*. Calcutta: University of Calcutta.

Jolly, Julius, ed. 1887. *Manu-smṛti: The Code of Manu*. London: Trubner.

Keith, Arthur Berriedale, trans. 1920. *Rigveda Brahmanas: The Aitareya and Kausitaki Brahmanas of the Rigveda*. Harvard Oriental Series, Vol. 25. Cambridge: Harvard University Press.

Kevalananda, Swami, and J. R. Gharpure, eds. *Manusmṛti with the Bhāṣya of Bhaṭṭa Medatithi*. Collections of Hindu Law Texts, No. 9. Poona: Aryasamskriti Mudranalaya.

Khare, G. H. 1936. "Krishnadevarāya of Vijayanagar and the Vitthala Image of Pandharpur." In *Vijayanagar Sexcentenary Commemoration Volume*. Dharwar: Vijayanagara Empire Sexcentenary Association.

Kielhorn, F. 1892. "Inscriptions from Khajurāho." *Epigraphia Indica* 1:121-52.

Krishna Sastri, H. 1912. "The Second Vijayanagar Dynasty; Its Viceroys and Ministers." *Annual Report. Archaeological Survey of India, 1908-09*. Calcutta: Government Printing.

________1920. "The Tiruvalangadu Copper-Plates of the Sixth Year Rājendra Chola I." *South Indian Inscriptions* 3:385-439.

________1923. *South Indian Inscriptions* 4.

Krishnan, K. G. 1984. *Karandai Tamil Sangam Plates of Rajendrachola I.* Memoirs of the Archaeological Survey of India, No. 79. Delhi: Archaeological Survey of India.

Krishanaswami Aiyangar, S. 1936. "The Character and Significance of the Empire of Vijayanagara in Indian History." In *Vijayanagara Sexentenary Commemoration Volume*. Dharwar: Vijayanagara Empire Sexentenary Association.

Longhurst, A. H. 1916-17. "Udayagiri Fort and Temple, Nellore District; The Krishna Temple at Vijayanagar." In *Annual Report of the Archaeological Department, Southern Circle. Madras. 1916-17.*

Madras Government Museum. 1951. *Centenary Souvenir (1851-1951).* Madras: Government Press.

Mirashi, V. V. 1955. "Bilhari Stone Inscriptions of Yuvarajadeva II." *Corpus Inscriptionum Indicarum* 4:204-24.

Mitter, Partha. 1977. *Much Maligned Monsters*. Oxford: Oxford University Press.

Nagaswamy, R. 1970. *Gangaikondacholapuram*. Madras: Tamilnadu State Department of Archaeology.

Nelson, J. H. 1868. *The Madura Country: A Manual*. Madras: Asylum Press.

Nilakanta Sastri, K. A., and N. Venkataramanayya. 1946. *Further sources of Vijayanagara History*. Madras: University of Madras.

Parker, Samuel. 1987. "Structure, History and Creativity in the Visual Arts: The Sarnath Asokan Pillar." Unpublished Essays. University of Chicago.

Pathak, K. B. 1907-8. "Kendur Plates of Kirtivarman II." *Epigraphia Indica* 9:200-6.

_______1909-10. "Rayagad Plates of Vijayāditya." *Epigraphia Indica* 10:14-17.

Sitaram Pandit, Ranjit, trans. 1935. *Rājataraṅgiṇī: The Saga of the Kings of Kashmir*. Allahabad: The Indian Press.

Sivaramamurthi, C. 1964a. *Nolamba Sculptures in the Madras Government Museum. Bulletin of the Madras Government Museum*, n.s. No. 9. Madras: Government of Madras.

________1964b. *Royal Conquest and Cultural Migrations in South India and the Deccan*. Calcutta: Indian Museum.

Sivasankara Pandiyaji, S. n.d. *Celebrations of the Navarātri Festival at Ramnad in 1892*. The Miniature Hindi Excelsior Series, Vol. 4. Madras: Adyar Theosophical Society Library.

Stein, Burton. 1983. "Mahanavami: Medieval and Modern Kingly Ritual in South India." In Bardwell Smith, ed., *Essays on Gupta Culture*. Delhi: Motilal Banarsidass.

Stein, M. A. , ed. 1892. *Kalhaṇa's Rājataraṅgiṇī or Chronicle of the Kings of Kashmir*. Bombay: Education Society's Press.

Tartakov, Gary, and Vidya Dehejia. 1984. "Sharing, Intrusion, and Influence: The Mahiṣāsuramardinī Imagery of the Cālukyas and the Pallavas." *Artibus Asiae* 45:287-345.

Taylor, William. 1835. *Oriental Historical Manuscripts*. Madras: C. J. Taylor.

Wickremasinghe, Don Martino De Zilva. 1912. "Jetavanarama Slab-Inscription (no. 1) of Mahinda IV." *Epigraphia Zeylanica* 1:213-29.

Williams, Joanna Gottfried. 1982. *The Art of Gupta India: Empire and Province*. Princeton: Princeton University Press.

Yule, Henry, and A. C. Burnell. [1903] 1968. *Hobson-Jobson*. Delhi: Munshiram Manoharlal.

Somanātha
Narratives of a History

Romila Thapar

Since the last two hundred years or so, the narrative of the raid of Maḥmūd of Ghazni on the temple of Somanātha has been derived from a single source – the Turko-Persian accounts. These speak of repeated raids on the temple and the killing of Hindus and Shi'as, suggesting that there was an immense resentment on the part of the Hindus against the Muslims. This then became the basis of arguing that the raid was seminal to the continuing antagonism between Hindus and Muslims in history culminating in the hatred between the two communities in the present day. Until recently there was a reliance on a single source and historians did not attempt to co-relate other texts that refer to Somanātha or to Maḥmūd.[1] Had this been done there would have been a rather different version of the history of Somanātha.

The attempt in this essay is to also enquire into these other sources and ascertain their perspectives on this history. Their

1 Among the writings that have extended the horizon and pointed to the importance of other sources are, A. K. Majumdar, *The Chaulukyas of Gujerat*, 1956; R. H. Davis, *Lives of Indian Images*, New Jersey 1997; Shahid Amin, "On Retelling the Muslim Conquest", in P. Chatterjee and Anjan Ghosh (ed.), *History and the Present*, 2002; M. C. Joshi, "Islam in the Hindu Tantra", *Journal of the Asiatic Society of Bombay*, 1983, pp. 51–56.

diversity is projected in the diversities of their histories. Even a juxtaposition of these sources presents a different view of the history of Somanātha. By focusing on the historiography of each source, not only do the many voices of the past become audible, but the nature of present day interpretations of the past, also become evident.

In 1026, Maḥmūd of Ghazni raided the temple of Somanātha and broke the idol. Reference is made to this in various sources, or, reference is omitted where one expects to find it. Some of the references contradict each other. Some lead to our asking questions which do not conform to what we have accepted so far in terms of the meaning and the aftermath of the event. The narrating of an event can get encrusted with interpretations from century to century and this changes the perception of the event. As historians therefore, we have to be aware not just of the event and how we look upon it today, but also the ways in which the event was interpreted through the intervening centuries. The analysis of these sources and the priorities in explanation stem of course from the historian's interpretation.

I would like to discuss some representations of this and other events at Somanātha, keeping in mind the historical question of how Maḥmūd's raid was viewed. They cover a wide span and are major representations. These are the accounts originating from Turko-Persian concerns, Jaina texts of the period, Sanskrit inscriptions from Somanātha, some popular perceptions, the debate in the British House of Commons and what is often described as a nationalist reading of the event.

Let me begin with a brief background to Somanātha itself. It is referred to in the *Mahābhārata* as *Prabhāsa*, and although it had no temple until later, it was a place of pilgrimage, a *tīrtha* – also associated with Kṛṣṇa and the Pāṇḍavas.[2] As was common to many parts of the sub-continent there were a variety of religious sects established in the area – Buddhist, Jaina, Śaiva and Muslim. Some existed in succession and some conjointly. The Śaiva temple, known

2 *Vana parvan* 13.14: 80. 78; 86. 18-19; 119.1.

bronze image of Śiva dancing on Nandi's back; and undoubtedly many more since removed by the plunderers (Balasubrahmanyam 1975; Nagaswamy 1970; Sivaramamurti 1964a). At the four entry gates of the fortified city, Rājendra placed images of the goddess Durgā or Kālī to act as guardians of the community within. One of the guardians, at least, was a Cālukyan conscript: a dramatic stone image of eight-armed Durgā defeating the Buffalo-demon, her left foot firmly planted on the back of the demon, who is on his knees and fading fast (illustration 6). Though the *pālī*-banner itself was no longer a target of imperial aspiration, the new capital Rājendra built was a sort of city-scale *pālī*-banner, with the tower of the Śiva temple looming over the rows of loot, insignia of the kings he had subordinated.

Destruction of Devotion

Of all modes of expropriation, certainly the most radical involves the destruction of images. Here it is not just a matter of change in proprietor but a radical transformation in form. The image is reduced to its material elements, denying or extinguishing any divine presence that may have inhabited it and risking in the process the possibility of divine retribution. Instead of continuing to exist as a second-order signifier, the object is at one moment deconstituted in an act powerful in rhetorical impact but limited in duration.

There is no question that medieval Hindu kings frequently destroyed religious images as part of more general rampages. When the Paramāras sacked the Rāṣṭrakūṭa capital of Mānyakheṭa or when the Colas leveled the Cālukya capital at Kalyāṇī we must presume that the many temples and images of those royal centers could not have been spared. However, Hindu narratives and inscriptions seldom describe destruction of images as a directed, politically meaningful act. (Abundant narratives of intentional image destruction come with the entry of Islam into the subcontinent, but that is another story.) When they do, they most often treat it as an extraordinary action, something morally ambiguous that may be justified only as the Somanātha temple at Prabhās, dates to about the ninth or tenth century AD.[3] The Caulukyas or Solankis were the ruling dynasty in Gujarat during the eleventh to thirteenth centuries. Kathiawar was administered by lesser *rājās* some of whom were subordinates of the Caulukyas.

Saurashtra was agriculturally fertile, but even more than that, its prosperity came from trade. The port at Somanātha, known as Veraval, was one of the three major ports of Gujarat. During this period western India had a conspicuously wealthy trade with ports along the Arabian peninsula and the Persian Gulf.[4] The antecedents of this trade go back many centuries. The Arab conquest of Sind was less indelible than the more permanent contacts based on trade. Arab traders and shippers settled along the west coast, married locally and were ancestors to many communities existing to the present. Some Arabs took employment with local rulers. Rāṣṭrakūṭa inscriptions speak of them as Tājika administrators and governors.[5] The counterparts to these Arab traders were Indian merchants based at Hormuz in Persia, and at Ghazni, who, even after the eleventh century, are described as extremely prosperous.[6]

The trade focused on the importing of horses from west Asia and also included wine, metal, textiles and spices. The most lucrative was the trade in horses.[7] Funds from temples formed a

3 B. K. Thapar, 'The Temple at Somanātha: History by Excavations', in K. M. Munshi, *Somnath: The Shrine Eternal*, Bombay, 1951, 71–90, 105–33; M.A. Dhaky and H. P. Sastri, *The Riddle of the Temple at Somanātha*, Varanasi, 1974.

4 V. K. Jain, 1990, *Trade and Traders in Western India*, Delhi.

5 *Epigraphia Indica*, XXXII, 47 ff.

6 Muhammad Ufi (sic), *Jami-ul-Hikayat*, in Elliot and Dowson, *The History of India as Told by its Own Historians* II, 201. Wasa Abhir from Anahilvada had property worth ten lakhs in Ghazni: impressive, even if exaggerated.

7 Abdullah Wassaf, *Tazjiyat-ul-Amsar*, in Elliot and Dowson, *The History of India as Told by its Own Historians* III, 31 ff. Marco Polo also comments on the wealth involved in the horse trade especially with southern India. *Prabandhacintāmaṇi*, 14; Rājaśekhara, *Prabandhakośa*, Shantiniketan, 1935, 121.

sizeable investment according to some sources.[8] Port towns such as Somanātha – Veraval and Cambay derived a handsome income from this trade, much of it doubtless being ploughed back to enlarge the profits. Apart from trade, another source of local income were the large sums of money collected in pilgrim taxes by the administration in Somanātha. This was a fairly common source of revenue for the same is mentioned in connection with the temple at Multan.[9] We are also told that the local *rājās* – the Cūḍasamas, Ābhīras, Yādavas and others – attacked the pilgrims and looted them of their donations intended for the Somanātha temple. In addition there was heavy piracy in the coastal areas indulged in by the local Chāvḍa *rājās* and a variety of sea brigands referred to as the Bawarij.[10] As with many areas generating wealth in earlier times, this part of Gujarat was also subject to unrest and the Caulukya administration spent much time and energy policing attacks on pilgrims and traders.

Despite all this, trade flourished. Gujarat in this period experienced what can perhaps be called a renaissance culture of the Jaina mercantile community. Rich merchant families were in political office, controlled state finances, were patrons of culture, were scholars of the highest order, were liberal donors to the Jaina *saṅgha* and builders of magnificent temples.

This is the backdrop as it were, to the Somanātha temple which by many accounts suffered a raid by Maḥmūd in 1026. There is one sober, contemporary reference and this comes not surprisingly, from Al-Bīrūnī, a central Asian scholar deeply interested in India, writing extensively on what he observed and learnt in the eleventh century. He tells us that there was a stone fortress built about a hundred years before Maḥmūd's raid, within which the *liṅgam* was located – presumably to safeguard the wealth of the temple. The idol was especially venerated by sailors and traders, not surprising

8 Abdullah Wassaf, Elliot and Dowson, *op.cit.*, I, 69; Pehoa Inscription, *Epigraphia Indica*, 1. 184 ff.

9 A. Wink, *Al-Hind*, volume 1, Delhi, 1990, 173 ff; 184 ff; 187 ff.

10 Alberuni in E. C. Sachau, *Alberuni's India*, New Delhi, 1964 (reprint), I.208.

considering the importance of the port at Veraval, trading as far as Zanzibar and China. He comments in a general way on the economic devastation caused by the many raids of Maḥmūd. Al-Bīrūnī also mentions that Durlabha of Multan, presumably a mathematician, used a round about way involving various eras, to compute the year of the raid on Somanātha as Śaka 947 (equivalent to AD 1025-6).[11] The raid, therefore, was known to local sources.

Not unexpectedly, the Turko-Persian chronicles indulge in elaborate myth-making around the event. A major poet of the eastern Islamic world, Farrukhī Sīstānī, who claims that he accompanied Maḥmūd to Somanātha, provides a fascinating explanation for the breaking of the idol.[12] This explanation has been largely dismissed by modern historians as too fanciful, but it has a significance for the assessment of iconoclasm. According to him the idol at Somanātha was not of a Hindu deity but of a pre-Islamic Arabian goddess. He tells us that the name Somnat (as it was often written in Persian) is actually, Sū-manāt – the place of Manāt. We know from the Qur'ān that Lāt, Uzza and Manāt were the three pre-Islamic goddesses widely worshipped,[13] and the destruction of their shrines and images it was said, had been ordered by the prophet Muhammad. Two were destroyed, but Manāt was believed to have been secreted away to Gujarat and installed in a place of worship. According to some descriptions Manāt was an aniconic block of black stone, so the form could be similar to a *liṅgam*. This story hovers over many of the Turko-Persian accounts, some taking it seriously, others being less emphatic and insisting instead that the icon was of a Hindu deity.

In the thirteenth century, the famous Persian poet Sa'dī provides a garbled description.[14] He claims to have visited the Somanātha

11 Ibid., II.9-10, 54.

12 F. Sīstānī in M. Nazim, *The Life and Times of Sultan Maḥmūd of Ghazni*, Cambridge 1931.

13 *Qur'ān*, 53. 19-20. G. Ryckmans, *Les Religions Arabes Pre-Islamique*, Louvain, 1951.

14 Sa'dī *Bustān* in A. H. Edwards, 1911, *The Bustān of Sa'dī*, London, 109.

temple, although there is no other mention of this. According to him the idol was of ivory and decorated like the idol of Manāt – a faultless, female form. Its hands moved magically, but when he secretly investigated this, it turned out that they were attached by string to the hands of a person standing behind the idol who worked their movements. According to him the rituals were conducted by priests who came from Iran. This is obviously the fantasy of a poet who has combined the story of Manāt, information on string puppets and rumours of some *brāhmaṇas* having associations with Iran and with the worship of the sun, perhaps confusing Somanātha with the sun-temple at Multan.

The identification of the Somanātha idol with that of Manāt has little historical credibility. There is no evidence to suggest that the temple housed an image of Manāt. Nevertheless the story is significant to the reconstruction of the aftermath of the event, since it is closely tied to the kind of legitimation which was being projected for Maḥmūd.

The link with Manāt added to the acclaim for Maḥmūd. Not only was he the prize iconoclast in breaking Hindu idols, but, in destroying Manāt, he had carried out what were said to be the very orders of the Prophet. He was therefore doubly a champion of Islam.[15] Other temples are raided by him and their idols broken, but Somanātha receives special attention in all the accounts of his activities. Writing of his victories to the Caliphate, Maḥmūd presents them as major accomplishments in the cause of Islam. And not surprisingly Maḥmūd becomes the recipient of grandiose titles. This establishes his legitimacy in the politics of the Islamic world, a dimension which is overlooked by those who see his activities only in the context of northern India.

But his legitimacy also derives from the fact that he was a Sunni Muslim and he attacked Ismā'īlīs and Shi'as whom the Sunnis

Quoted in R. H. Davis, *Lives of Indian Images*, New Jersey, 1997, 100 ff.

15 Nazim, *op. cit.*

regarded as heretics.[16] It was ironic that the Ismā'īlīs attacked the temple of Multan and were in turn attacked by Maḥmūd in the eleventh century and their mosque was shut down. The fear of the heretic was due to the popularity of heresies against orthodox Islam and political hostility to the Caliphate in the previous couple of centuries, none of which would be surprising given that Islam in these areas was a relatively new religion. Maḥmūd is said to have desecrated their places of worship at Multan and Manṣūra. His claims to having killed fifty thousand *kāfir*s – infidels, is matched by similar claims to his having killed fifty thousand Muslim heretics. The figure appears to be notional. Maḥmūd's attacks on the Hindus and on the Shi'as and Ismā'īlīs, was a religious crusade against the infidel and the heretic. But interestingly, these were also the places and peoples involved in the highly profitable horse trade with the Arabs and the Gulf. Both the Muslim heretics of Multan and the Hindu traders of Somanātha had substantial commercial investments. Is it possible then that Maḥmūd, in addition to religious iconoclasm, was also trying to terminate the import of horses to India via Sind and Gujarat? This would have curtailed the Arab monopoly over the trade. Given the fact that there was a competitive horse trade with Afghanistan through north-western India, which was crucial to the wealth of the state of Ghazni, Maḥmūd may well have been combining iconoclasm with trying to obtain a commercial advantage.[17]

In the subsequent and multiple Persian accounts – and there are many in each century – the contradictions and exaggerations increase. There is no agreement on the form of the image. Some say that it is a *liṅgam*, others reverse this and describe it as anthropomorphic – a human form.[18] But even with this there is no

16 Wink, *op. cit.*, 184-9; 217-18.

17 Cf. Mohammad Habib, *Sultan Maḥmūd of Ghazni*, Delhi, 1967.

18 Ibn Attar quoted in Nazim, op. cit.; Ibn Asir in *Gazetteer of the Bombay Presidency*, I, 523; Elliot and Dowson, II, 248 ff; 468 ff. Al-Kazwini, Elliot and Dowson, I, 97 ff. Abdullah Wassaf, Elliot and Dowson, III, 44 ff; IV. 181.

consistency as to whether it is a female Manāt or a male Śiva. There seems to have been almost a lingering wish that it might be Manāt. Was the icon, if identified with Manāt, more important perhaps to Muslim sentiment?

The anthropomorphic form encouraged stories of the nose being knocked off and the piercing of the belly from which jewels poured forth.[19] Fantasizing on the wealth of the temples evoked a vision of immense opulence, and this could suggest that the Turkish raids were a veritable 'gold-rush'.[20] One account states that the image contained twenty *man* of jewels – one *man* weighing several kilograms; another, that a gold chain weighing two hundred *man* kept the image in place. Yet another describes the icon as made of iron with a magnet placed above it, so that it would be suspended in space, an awesome sight for the worshipper.[21] The age of the temple is taken further and further back in time until it is described as thirty thousand years old. One wonders if Somanātha was not becoming something of a fantasy in such accounts.

More purposive writing of the fourteenth century are the chronicles of Baranī and 'Iṣāmī. Both were associated with courts, one with the Delhi Sultanate and the other with the Bahmani kingdom of the Deccan. Both project Maḥmūd as the ideal Muslim ruler, but somewhat differently. Baranī states that his writing is intended to educate Muslim rulers in their duties towards Islam.[22] For him, religion and kingship are twins and the ruler needs to know the religious ideals of kingship if he claims to be ruling on behalf of God. Sultans must protect Islam through the *sharī'a* and destroy both Muslim heretics and infidels. Maḥmūd is said to be the ideal ruler because he did both.

19 Attar quoted in Nazim, op. cit., 221; Firishta in J. Briggs, *History of the Rise of the Mohammadan Power in India*, Calcutta, 1996 (reprint).

20 A. Wink, *Al-Hind*, volume II, 124 ff.

21 Zakariya al-Kazwini, *Asar ul-Bilad*, Elliot and Dowson, *op. cit.*, I, 97 ff.

22 *Fatāwā-yi-Jahāndārī* discussed in P. Hardy, *Historians of Medieval India*, Delhi, 1997 (repr.), 25 ff; 107 ff.

'Iṣāmī composes what he regards as an epic poem on the Muslim rulers of India, on the lines of the famous Persian poet Firdausī's earlier epic on the Persian kings, the *Shāh-nāma*. 'Iṣāmī argues that kingship descended from God, first to the pre-Islamic rulers of Persia – in which he includes Alexander of Macedon and the Sassanid kings, and subsequently to the Sultans of India, with Maḥmūd establishing Muslim rule in India.[23] Interestingly the Arabs, who had both a political and economic presence in the subcontinent prior to Maḥmūd, hardly figure in this history. That there is a difference of perception in these narratives, is important to a historical assessment and requires further investigation.

The role of Maḥmūd it would seem, was undergoing a change from being viewed merely as an iconoclast to also being projected as the founder of an Islamic state in India, even if the latter statement was not historically accurate. Presumably given his status in Islamic historiography this was a form of indirectly legitimizing the Sultans in India. The appropriation of the pre-Islamic Persian rulers for purposes of legitimacy, suggests that there may have been an element of doubt about the accepted role models of Muslim rulers. The Sultans in India were not only ruling a society substantially of non-Muslims, but even those who had converted to Islam were in large part following the customary practices of their *zāt*, their erstwhile Hindu caste, which were often not in conformity with the *sharī'a*. Is there then a hint of an underlying uncertainty, of a lack of confidence, in the insistence on taking Islamic rule back to Maḥmūd, a champion of the Islamic world? Can we say that these accounts had converted the event itself at Somanātha, into what some today would call, an icon?

In the post-fourteenth century, narratives of the event continue with still greater embellishments and these are perhaps what we would see as a cloud of hype. Of the actual temple the impression sought to be created is that it never recovered from the raid and ceased to be important. Yet every few decades some Sultan is

23 *Futūḥ-al-Salāṭīn* discussed in Hardy, *op. cit.*, 107-8.

said to have attacked the Somanātha temple and converted it into a mosque.[24] Logically therefore, and logic is not at a premium in these accounts, they would, after the first attack, be attacking a mosque. In a sense the claim ceases to be history and becomes rhetoric. Nor does this stop Sanskrit texts from continuing to refer to it as a temple, a holy city, a second Kailāśa.[25] Was this a parallel situation to the mosque-church toggle-switching at places such as Cordoba in Spain and Santa Sophia in Istanbul, each time the area changed rulers or a religion receded?

Let me turn now to the Jaina texts of this period. These, not unexpectedly associate a different set of concerns with the event, or else they ignore it. The eleventh century Jaina poet from the Paramāra court in Malwa, Dhanapāla, a contemporary of Maḥmūd, briefly mentions Maḥmūd's campaign in Gujarat and his raids on various places including Somanātha.[26] He comments however, at much greater length on Maḥmūd's inability to damage the icons of Mahāvīra in Jaina temples for, as he puts it, snakes cannot swallow Garuḍa nor can stars dim the light of the sun. This for him is proof of the superior power of the Jaina images as compared to the Śaiva, the latter having been descecrated.

In the early twelfth century, another Jaina text informs us that the Caulukya king, angered by the *rākṣasa*s, the *daitya*s and the *asura*s who were destroying temples and disturbing the *ṛṣi*s and *brāhmaṇa*s, campaigned against them.[27] One expects the list to include the Turuṣkas as the Turks were called, but instead mention is made of the local *rājā*s. The king is said to have made

24 Dhaky and Sastri, *op. cit.*

25 *Ibid.*

26 *Satyapurīya-Mahāvīra-utsaha*, III.2. D. Sharma, 'Some New Light on the Route of Mahmud of Ghazni's Raid on Somanatha: Multan to Somanatha and Somanatha to Multan', in B. P. Sinha (ed.), *Dr. Satkari Mookerji Felicitation Volume*, Varanasi, 1969, 165-8.

27 Hemachandra, *Dvyāśrāya-kāvya*, in *Indian Antiquary* 1875, 4, 72 ff, 110 ff, 232 ff, 265 ff; *Ibid.*; J. Klatt, 'Extracts from the Historical Records of the Jainas', *Indian Antiquary* 1882, 11, 245-56.

a pilgrimage to Somanātha and found that the temple was old and was disintegrating. He is said to have stated that it was a disgrace that the local *rājā*s were plundering pilgrims but could not keep the temples in good repair. This is the same king who built a mosque at Cambay, which mosque was later destroyed in a campaign against the Caulukyas of Gujarat by the Paramāras of Malwa. But the Paramāra king also looted the Jaina and other temples built under the patronage of the Caulukyas.[28] It would seem that when the temple was seen as a statement of power, it could become a target of attack, irrespective of religious affiliations.

In the late twelfth century during the reign of the famous Caulukya king, Kumārapāla, there is much activity around the Somanātha temple. Among the ministers of Kumārapāla was Hemacandra, a respected and erudite scholar of Jaina religious history, and incidentally a rival of the Śaiva Pāśupata chief priest of the Somanātha temple, Bhāva Bṛhaspati. Such Śaiva-Jaina rivalry was known to other parts of the sub-continent as well. There is therefore some discrepancy between the statements of the minister and chief priest.

Various Jaina texts, giving the history of Kumārapāla mention his connection with Somanātha. It is stated that he wished to be immortalized.[29] So Hemacandra persuaded the king to replace the dilapidated temple at Somanātha with a new stone temple. The temple is clearly described as dilapidated and not destroyed having fallen into disrepair because of weathering from seaspray. When the new temple on the location of the old had been completed, both Kumārapāla and Hemacandra took part in the ritual of consecration. Hemacandra wished to impress the king with the spiritual powers of a Jaina *ācārya*, so on his bidding, Śiva, the deity of the temple, appeared before the king. Kumārapāla was so overcome by this

28 P. Bhatia, *The Paramaras*, Delhi, 1970, 141.

29 Meruṭunga, *Prabandha-cintāmaṇi*, 4.9.140ff, C. H. Tawney (trans.), Calcutta, 1899, IV, 129 ff. G. Buhler, *The Life of Hemacandracarya*, Shantiniketan, 1936.

miracle that he converted to the Jaina faith. The focus again is on the superior power of Jainism over Śaivism. The renovating of the temple which is also important, takes on the symbolism of political legitimation for the king. It does seem curious that these activities focused on the Somanātha temple, yet no mention is made of Maḥmūd, in spite of the raid having occurred in the previous couple of centuries. The miracle is the central point in the connection with Somanātha in these accounts.

Some suggestions of an anguish over what may be indirect references to the raids of Maḥmūd come from quite other Jaina sources and interestingly these relate to the merchant community. In an anthology of stories, one refers to the merchant Jāvaḍi, who quickly makes a fortune in trade and then goes in search of a Jaina icon which had been taken away to the land called Gajjana.[30] This is clearly Ghazna. The ruler of Gajjana was a Yavana – a term by now used for those coming from the west. The Yavana ruler was easily won over by the wealth presented to him by Jāvaḍi. He allowed Jāvaḍi to search for the icon and when it was found, gave him permission to take it back. Not only that but the Yavana worshipped the icon prior to its departure. The second part of the narrative deals with the vicissitudes of having the icon installed in Gujarat, but that is another story.

This is a reconciliation story with a certain element of wishful thinking. The initial removal of the icon is hurtful and creates anguish. Its return should ideally be through reconciling iconoclasts to the worship of icons. There are other touching stories in which the ruler of Gajjana or other Yavana kings are persuaded not to attack Gujarat. But such stories are generally related as a demonstration of the power of the Jaina *ācārya*s.

The Jaina sources therefore underline their own ideology. Jaina temples survive, Śaiva temples get destroyed. Śiva has abandoned his icons unlike Mahāvīra who still resides in his icons and protects

30 P. Granoff, 'The Householder as Shaman: Jaina Biographies of Temple Builders', *East and West*, 42, 1992, 2-4, 301-17; R. Davis, *op.cit.*, 194–96.

them. Attacks are to be expected in the Kaliyuga – the present age – since it is an age of evil. Icons will be broken but wealthy Jaina merchants will restore the temple and the icons will invariably and miraculously, mend themselves.

The argument about Kaliyuga and iconoclasm also occurs in the *Purāṇa*s, where an increasing decline in *dharma* accompanies the passing of the cycle of time. Deities desert their icons in the Kaliyuga especially if kings are not attentive enough to them.[31] Sometimes there is a mention of temples being destroyed but generally they are said to have been dilapidated and neglected – as would be expected in an age of declining virtue – and therefore requiring repair. The association with Kaliyuga gives the situation a feeling of infallibility. Kaliyuga is therefore a partial but generalized reference to the vulnerability of the practice and symbol of *dharma*. What remains curious is the lack of specific mention about Maḥmūd's raid on Somanātha, which in the Turko-Persian chronicles is so central.

The third category of major narratives is constituted by the inscriptions in Sanskrit from Somanātha itself, focusing on the temple and the vicinity. These are perhaps the most important sources and have been frequently cited and read since the late nineteenth century, but seldom in the context of local history. The perspectives which these point to are again very different from the earlier two sources. In the twelfth century the Caulukya king, Kumārapāla, issues an inscription. He appoints a governor to protect Somanātha and the protection is against the piracy and the looting by the local *rājā*s.[32] A century later, the Caulukyas are again protecting the site, this time from attacks by the Malwa *rājā*s.[33] The

31 P. Granoff, 'Tales of Broken Limbs and Bleeding Wounds: Responses to Muslim Iconoclasm in Medieval India', *East and West*, 41, 1991, 1-4, 182-203. *Vāyu Purāṇa*, I. 58. 31-74; II. 36. 115-25.

32 Praci Inscription, *Poona Orientalist*, 1937, 1.4. 39-46.

33 *Epigraphia Indica*, II, 437 ff.

regular complaint about local *rājās* looting pilgrims at Somanātha becomes a continuing refrain in many inscriptions.

In 1169, an inscription records the appointment of the chief priest of the Somanātha temple, Bhāva Bṛhaspati.[34] He claims to have come from Kannauj, from a family of Pāśupata Śaiva *brāhmaṇas* and, as the inscriptions show, initiated a succession of powerful priests at the Somanātha temple. He states that he was sent by Śiva himself to rehabilitate the temple. This was required because it was an old structure, much neglected by the wicked and greedy officers and because temples in any case deteriorate in the Kaliyuga. Bhāva Bṛhaspati claims that it was he who persuaded Kumārapāla to replace the older wooden temple with a stone temple.

Again no mention is made of the raid of Maḥmūd. Was this out of embarrassment, that a powerful icon of Śiva had been desecrated? Or was the looting of a temple not such an extraordinary event? The Turko-Persian chronicles may well have been indulging in exaggeration. Yet the looting of the pilgrims by the local *rājās* is repeatedly mentioned. Was Kumārapāla's renovation both an act of veneration of Śiva but also a seeking of legitimation? Was this in a sense an inversion of Maḥmūd seeking legitimation through raiding the temple? Are these then counter-points of legitimation in viewing the past?

In 1264, a long legal document was issued in the form of an inscription with both a Sanskrit and an Arabic version and concerns the acquisition of land and the building of a mosque by a trader from Hormuz.[35] Being a legal document it was dated in four current dating systems – Hijrī, Saṁvat, Siṁha and Valabhī. The Sanskrit version begins with the usual formulaic symbol – the *siddham* – and continues with invoking Viśvanātha, a name for Śiva. But there is also a suggestion that it was a rendering into Sanskrit of Allah, the lord of the Universe. The parallel is striking at more than one place in the inscription and can be viewed as yet another

34 Prabhaspattana Inscription, *BPSI*, 186, vs. 4, 11, 17-18.

35 Somanathapattana Veraval Inscription, *Epigraphia Indica*, XXXIV, 141ff.

example of cultural translation. We are told that Khoja Noradina Piroja/Nuruddin Feroz, the son of Khoja Nau Abu Brahima of Hurmujadeśa/Hormuz, a *nakhuda* or commander of a ship, a *sadr*/ chief and evidently a respected trader – as his title Khoja/Khwaja, would indicate – acquired land in Mahājanapālī on the outskirts of the town of Somanātha, to build a mosque, which is referred to as a *mijigiti*/*masjid*, and described as a *dharmasthāna*. The land was acquired from the local *rājā*, Śrī Chāḍā, son of Nānasiṁha, and reference is also made to the governor of Kathiawar, the *mahāmātya* Māladeva, and the Caulukya-Vaghela king, Arjunadeva.

The acquisition of this land has the approval of two local bodies – the *pañcakula* and the association of the *jamātha*. The *pañcakula*s were powerful administrative and local committees, well established by this period, consisting of recognized authorities such as priests, officers, merchants, local dignitaries. This particular *pañcakula* was headed by the Para/*purohita* Vīrabhadra, the Śaiva Pāśupata *ācārya* most likely of the Somanātha temple, and among its members was the merchant Abhaysiṁha. From other inscriptions it would seem that Para Vīrabhadra was related to Bhāva Bṛhaspati in a line of succession. The witnesses to this agreement of granting land for the building of the mosque are mentioned by name and described as the *bṛhat-puruṣa*, literally 'the big men'. They were the *Ṭhakkura*s, *Rāṇaka*s, *Rājā*s and merchants, many from the Mahājanapālī. Some of these dignitaries were functionaries of the estates of the Somanātha and other temples. The land given for the mosque in Mahājanapālī was part of these estates.

The other committee endorsing the agreement was the *jamātha*, consisting of ship-owners, artisans, sailors and religious teachers, probably from Hormuz. Also mentioned are the oil-millers, masons and Musalmāna horse-handlers, all referred to by what appear to be occupational or caste names, such as *cūnākāra* and *ghamcika*. Were these local converts to Islam? Since the *jamātha* was to ensure these endowments for the maintenance of the mosque, it was necessary to indicate its membership.

The inscription lists the endowments for the mosque. These included two large measures of land which were part of the temple property from adjoining temples situated in Somanātha-pattana; land from a *maṭha*; income from two shops in the vicinity; and an oil mill. The measures of land were bought from the *purohita* and the chief priests of the temples and the sales were attested by the men of rank. The shops and the oil-mill were purchased from the local people. One of the chief priests, Tripurāntaka, seems to appear again, twenty-three years later, in a number of inscriptions as a wealthy and powerful Pāśupata Śaiva priest who built many temples in the vicinity.[36] As with many Sanskrit votive inscriptions, it ends with the hope that the terms and conditions of the agreement may last as long as the moon and sun endure.

The tone and sentiment of the inscription is amicable and clearly the settlement had been agreed to on all sides. The building of a substantial mosque in association with some of the properties of the Somanātha temple, not by a conqueror but by a trader through a legal agreement, was obviously not objected to, neither by the local governor and dignitaries nor by the priests, all of whom were party to the decision. The mosque is thus closely linked to the erstwhile properties and the functionaries of the Somanātha temple.

This raises many questions. Did this transaction, two hundred or so years after the raid of Maḥmūd, not interfere with the remembrance of the raid as handed down, in the minds of the priests and the local 'big men'? Were memories short or was the event relatively unimportant?

Nuruddin Feroz used Sanskrit and Arabic for the agreement, Sanskrit as the local formal language and Arabic probably as the language of incoming traders. The two texts are by and large similar but not identical. The Arabic version carries the hope that the people of Somanātha will convert to Islam – a statement which is wisely deleted in the Sanskrit version. The use of Arabic points to a specific identity distinct from the use of Persian in connection

36 The Cintra *Praśasti*, *Epigraphia Indica*, I, 271 ff.

with Maḥmūd. Did the local people make a distinction between the Arab and west Asian traders on the one hand – often referred to as Tājikas, and the Turks or Turuṣkas on the other? And were the former acceptable and the Turks much less so? Clearly they were not all homogenized and identified as 'Muslims', as we would do today. Should we not sift the reactions to the event by examining the responses of particular social groups and situations? Hormuz was crucial to the horse trade, therefore Nuruddin was welcomed. Did the profits of trade over-rule other considerations? Were the temples and their administrators also investing in horse trading and making handsome profits?

In the fifteenth century a number of short inscriptions from Gujarat refer to the battles against the Turks. One very moving inscription in Sanskrit comes from Somanātha itself.[37] Although written in Sanskrit, it begins with the Islamic formulaic blessing – *bismillāh ir-raḥmān ir-raḥīm*. It gives details of the family of the Vohara/Bohra Farīd who were of Arab descent. We are told that the town of Somanātha was attacked by the Turuṣkas, the Turks, and Vohara Farīd who was the son of Vohara Muḥammad, joined in the defence of the town, fighting against the Turuṣkas on behalf of the local ruler Brahmadeva. Farīd was killed and the inscription is a memorial to him.

The received opinion is that events such as the raid on Somanātha created what have been called two antagonistic categories of epic: the "epics of conquest" written in Persian to glorify Muslim rule and the "counter-epics of resistance" written in Hindi, Rajasthani/ Gujarati, to highlight Hindu resistance to the Muslims.[38] This statement is frequently accepted but requires some further analysis.[39]

37 D. B. Diskalkar, 'Inscriptions of Kathiawad', *New Indian Antiquary*, 1939, 1, 591.

38 Aziz Ahmed, "Epic and Counter-Epic in Medieval India," *Journal of the American Oriental Society, 1963*, 83, 470–76.

39 Davis, *op.cit.*, 89 ff. For a different perspective see, R. Sreenivasan, "Alaudin Khalji Remembered: Conquest, Gender and Community in Medieval Rajput Narratives," *Studies in History,2002*, ns 18, 2, 275-96.

The counter-epics of resistance are said to be the poems on the heroic deeds of Pṛthvīrāja Chauhan resisting Muḥammad Ghūrī as also those featuring the events, later in time, of the reign of 'Alā'-ud-dīn Khaljī, such as the *Kanhadāde Prabandha* and the *Hammīramahākāvya*.

The hostility in the Pṛthvīrāja poems appears to be more that of the Rajput for the Turk and vice versa, than that of the Hindu for the Muslim. The battle was over territory and it was the territory of the Chauhans that the Turks were trying to conquer. The epics on Pṛthvīrāja such as the *Pṛthvīrāja-rāso* of Chand Bardai and the *Pṛthvīrāja-vijaya* of Jayanaka, were in the style of eulogies as were many such courtly poems and were not intended primarily as factual accounts. Poets therefore took liberties as did Chand Bardai in narrating the captivity and death of Pṛthvīrāja. As in much courtly literature there is an overlay of exaggeration that has to be pared away.

The start of the narrative is often stereo-typical where disloyalty to the Rajput king by a high-ranking advisor reflects on how the hostilities begin. Mention is made of a minister, often a *brāhmaṇa*, who is slighted by the Rajput king and therefore defects to the Turkish side and assists the Turkish ruler to conquer the Chauhan domain. Meruṭuṅga's *Prabandhacintāmaṇi* has a variant version from those usually quoted such as the *Pṛthvīrāja-rāso* and the *Pṛthvīvijaya*. Meruṭuṅga relates that Someśvara, the minister of Pṛthvīrāja, tried to dissuade the king from going into battle against the *mlecchas*, presumably the Turks. The king insulted him so the minister joined the *mlecchas*. Pṛthvīrāja lost the battle and was captured, but the *mleccha* king decided to reinstate him. On arriving at the Chauhan capital, the *mleccha* king saw paintings of pigs killing the *mlecchas* and this so incensed him that he had Pṛthvīrāja killed.[40] It could be argued that this narrative points to hostility between the Hindu king and the Muslim Sultan, but it points also to a confrontation between

40 *Prabandhacintāmaṇi* 5.11.216.

the *brāhmaṇa* minister and the *kṣatriya* ruler, a confrontation not unknown to the politics of Rajput courts.

The epics relating to 'Alā'-ud-dīn Khaljī are different in tone and narrative. The role of the Turks had changed as they were now not merely seeking to conquer territory but were asserting themselves as the established rulers seeking to extend their administrative control. The conflict is now a Chauhan-Khalji competition for power. The story in the *Kanhadāde Prabandha* also begins with the betrayal by a *brāhmaṇa* minister.[41] 'Alā'-ud-dīn's general returns with the *liṅgam* from the Somanātha temple, but it is rescued en route to Delhi by the Rajput ruler of Jalor. (However, the account of Baranī writing from Delhi differs, as according to him the *liṅgam* was brought to Delhi and displayed in the capital, presumably as a trophy).[42] Curiously there is no reference to the earlier Turkish attack on the temple by Maḥmūd. Despite the hostility towards the Turk much of the epic focuses on other matters, including a proposal of marriage sent by 'Alā'-ud-dīn whose daughter wishes to marry the prince of Jalor. She recalls at length the many previous births when they were married. The prince rejects the proposal as it would bring dishonour to the Rajput, but it is unclear as to whether the dishonour was because he would be marrying the daughter of a current enemy or because as a Muslim she was a *mleccha* in terms of her caste identity.

According to the *Hammīramahākāvya,* the Rajput ruler of Ranthambhor, Hammīra, was attacked by 'Alā'-ud-dīn, because he gave shelter to the Mongol Muslims hostile to the Turks and because he had failed to pay the annual tribute.[43] Refusal to pay the

41 K. D.Vyas, (ed.), *Kanhadāde Prabandha,* Jaipur 1953; V. S.Bhatnagar (trans.), Delhi 1991; D. Sharma, *Early Chauhan Dynasties,* Delhi 1975 (2nd.ed.).

42 Ẓiyā'-al-Dīn Baranī, *Ta'rīkh-i-Fīrūz Shāhī,* ed. Saiyid Ahmed Khan, Calcutta, 1862, 251-3; P. Jackson, *The Delhi Sultanate: A Political History,* Cambridge 1999, 80-81.

43 *Hammīramahākāvya,* IX. 1–27; 39–47; X. 8-10; 88: XI. 1-2; XIII. 69–166. The name Hammīra has its own interest. It is a Sanskritic rendering of the title Amir used for chiefs and rulers. Maḥmūd for instance, is often given this title. That

annual tribute can be read as resistance but this kind of resistance would have existed in pre-Islamic times as well. That he was close to the Mongol Muslims again points to a political opposition to the Khaljīs rather than one based solely on religion. Only a third of the *Hammīramahākāvya* deals with this confrontation, the rest relating his campaigns against various Rajput rulers and their mutual hostilities. Most of Hammīra's Rajput ministers and officers of rank double-crossed him and joined 'Alā'-ud-dīn, but the one who remained loyal to the end was his Mongol Muslim minister. It has been argued that the question of loyalty and disloyalty was more central to many of these relationships than religious affiliations alone.[44]

These are the poems that have been quoted as epics of Hindu resistance but they hardly conform to this description. In essence they continue the earlier pre-Islamic tradition of the *carita*s or biographies of kings, and they endorse the values of the culture of royal courts. Wherever campaigns are conducted the enemy is described in as much gory detail as are the Turks in these accounts. There were some occasions when the hostility was expressed in religious terms but more often there were other reasons and concerns for hostility. To argue therefore that these were epics drawing largely, if not only, on religious resistance, seems unconvincing.

There are other voices that have so far been ignored by historians but which are now beginning to be heard. References to Maḥmūd or his nephew in popular narratives take an unexpected turn and provide reflections on these events that are different from the received version. A text that is generally regarded as spurious by historians, refers to a certain Sālār Mas'ūd as a nephew of Maḥmūd. There is little evidence for such a person. But what is of interest is that the narrative of his supposed early life as a phenomenal conquering general was set aside in the popular tradition and he

a number of Rajputs took this name suggests some admiration for the Turks.

44 B. Metcalf, "Too Little and Too Much: Reflections on Muslims in the History of India," *Journal of Asian Studies*, 1995, 54,4, 951-967.

emerged as the widely worshipped *pīr* of northern India, Ghāzī Miyān.[45] Among the most frequently repeated stories about him is the one that relates his death as occurring when he was called upon to prevent a local raja from killing a herd of cows belonging to the Ahirs. This story is associated with other local leaders, but what is significant that it is particularly known in connection with Ghāzī Miyān.

In the interface between Hinduism and Islam during the period after the fourteenth century, the most widely prevalent religious forms that emerged were those of the Bhakti *sants*, the Nathapanthis and Sakta groups and Sufi sects. In the tradition of Gorakhanatha and in some Tantric compositions, such as the *Śābara Tantra*, Maḥmūd is invoked and his name occurs among those of *pīr*s and gurus.[46] These perceptions and the concerns of their authors were strikingly different from those that are generally quoted from the Persian chronicles.

It would seem from these sources that the aftermath of the raid of Maḥmūd took the form of varying perceptions of the event and different from what has been previously assumed, particularly as seminal to a continuing Hindu-Muslim antagonism. How then have we arrived today at the rather simplistic historical theory that the raid of Maḥmūd created a trauma in the Hindu consciousness which has been at the root of Hindu-Muslim relations ever since. Or to put it in the words of K. M. Munshi writing in 1951 and referring to Somanātha and the Hindus, "For a thousand years Maḥmūd's destruction of the shrine has been burnt into the collective subconscious of the race as an unforgettable national disaster."[47]

---

45 Shahid Amin, " On Retelling the Muslim Conquest," *op.cit.*, 24–43; T. Mahmood, "The Dargah of Sayyid Salar Mas'ud Ghazi in Bahraich: Legend, Tradition and Reality", and I. H. Siddiqui, "A Note on the Dargah of Salar Mas'ud in Bahraich in the Light of Standard Historical Sources", in C. W. Troll (ed.), *Muslim Shrines in India,* 24–47.

46 M. C. Joshi, "Islam in the Hindu Tantras", *Journal of the Asiatic Society of Bombay,* 1983, 51–56.

47 K. M. Munshi, *Somanatha: the Shrine Eternal,* 58.

Interestingly what appears to be the earliest mention of a "Hindu trauma" in connection with Maḥmūd's raid on Somanātha, comes from the debate in the British Parliament in London in 1843, on the question of the gates of the Somanātha temple.[48] In 1842, the Governor-General of India, Lord Ellenborough, issued his famous Proclamation of the gates, in which he ordered the general in charge of the British army in Afghanistan, to return via Ghazni and bring back to India the sandalwood gates from the tomb of Maḥmūd. These were believed to have been looted from Somanātha. It was claimed that the intention was to return what was looted from India, an act which symbolized British control over Afghanistan despite their poor showing in the Anglo-Afghan wars. It was also presented as an attempt to reverse Indian subjugation to Afghanistan in the pre-British period.

The Proclamation raised a storm in the House of Commons and became a major issue in the cross-fire between the Government and the Opposition. The question was asked whether Ellenborough was catering to religious prejudices by appeasing the Hindus, or, was he appealing to national sympathies? It was also argued that no historian mentions the gates in the various accounts of Maḥmūd's raid, therefore the story of the gates could only be a fabrication which Ellenborough foolishly took as history. Where the story of the gates came from remains a mystery although there are some associations with the demands made by Ranjit Singh who was then ruling in the Punjab, from the king of Afghanistan.[49] But Ranjit Singh does not appear to have been very clear about which gates he was demanding and this may have been merely a bargaining point with the king of Afghanistan.

The chronicles in Persian written at the courts of the Sultans and the Mughals were taken as relatively reliable history by British

---

48 *The United Kingdom House of Commons Debate, March 9 1943,* on, The Somnath [Prabhas Patan] Proclamation, Junagarh 1948, 548-602, 630-32, 656, 674. See also, Davis, 197ff.

49 M. Yapp, *Strategies of British India,* Oxford 1980, 443-4.

historians. Their form was familiar to colonial historians and they were suggestive of the essentials of nineteenth century historical writing in their concern for chronology and sequential narrative and in their treatment of politically important events. There was little interest in questioning the ideological perspective of these narratives. In propagating the greatness of Muslim rulers they may well have exaggerated and dramatized the power of such rulers over their subjects. The exaggeration could have been occasioned by an actually tenuous relationship between ruler and subject, characteristic even of political conditions in some Indian power centers of earlier times. Among the narratives describing the event, the British were perhaps most familiar with the account of the seventeenth century historian Ferishta as this had been rendered into English by Alexander Dow in the eighteenth century in his *History of Hindustan*. Ferishta's account was as fanciful as the earlier ones, but now with further obvious exaggerations. Nevertheless it became the accepted version. A further dimension to the Hindu-Muslim dichotomy was expressed by James Mill through his periodisation of Indian history into Hindu civilization, Muslim civilization and the British period. In his hegemonic *History of British India,* published in the early nineteenth century and extensively read, Mill insists not only on the innate hostility of Hindu and Muslim, but also on the tyranny of the Muslim over the Hindu and the oppression of the Hindu by the Muslim. Mill had neither visited India nor read anything substantial on Indian history. The colonial interest in emphasizing this view is clearly stated in the Introduction to Elliot and Dowson's *History of India as Told by its Own Historians,* where it is said that the Hindus have to recognize that British rule is far superior for them than the rule of the Muslims.[50]

Given this background even members of the House of Commons saw the relations between the Hindus and Muslims as dichotomous and were also using their perceptions of Indian history as ammunition in their own political and party hostilities.

50 Elliot and Dowson, *op.cit.*, Vol.1.

Those critical of Ellenborough were fearful of the consequences: they saw the fetching of the gates as supporting a native religion, and that too the monstrous Linga-ism as they called it; and they felt that its political consequences would be violent indignation among the Muslims. Those supporting Ellenborogh argued equally vehemently that he was removing the feeling of degradation from the minds of the Hindus: that "it would relieve that country which had been overrun by the Mohammadan conqueror, from the painful feelings which had been rankling amongst the people for nearly a thousand years." The memory of the gates were thought to have been a painful memorial of the most devastating invasions that had ever desolated the country. The gates were uprooted and brought back but were found to be of non-Indian origin and in fact not associated with India.[51]

The more significant question is that of the wider implications of this debate on the Indian people. Did this debate fan an anti-Muslim Hindu sentiment among Hindus in India, which, judging from the earlier sources, had either not existed or had been marginal and localized? The absence in earlier times of an articulation of a trauma remains enigmatic. Historians have commented on the fact that there is no reference to the raid of Maḥmūd in non-Persian sources from India.[52]

From this point on, the arguments of the debate in the House of Commons come to be reflected in the writing on Somanātha. Maḥmūd's raid became a central point in Hindu-Muslim relations. K. M. Munshi led the demand for the restoration of the Somanātha temple soon after Indian independence in 1947. His wish to highlight the glories of Hindu history began in a general way with his writing historical novels and he then turned to eulogizing the Aryan glory of the pre-Islamic past. Historical novels became fashionable in India with Walter Scott and Alexander Dumas providing the models.

51 J. Fergusson, *A History of Indian and Eastern Architecture, 2* vols., London 1910 (revised ed.) Vol.2., 192.

52 A. K. Majumdar, *Chaulukyas of Gujarat,* Bombay 1956, 43.

Munshi's historical novel, *Jaya Somanātha,* was published in 1937. It is thought that some touches of Bankim Chandra Chatterjee's *Ānandamaṭha* are discernable in Munshi's novel. And as one historian, R. C. Majumdar puts it, Bankim Chandra's nationalism was Hindu rather than Indian, with passionate outbursts against the subjugation of India by the Muslims,[53] although this did not prevent him from expressing anti-colonial sentiments when he chose to. Munshi's comments in his book, *Somanatha – The Shrine Eternal,* sometimes echo the statements made in the British Parliament.

His insistence that the temple be restored was preceded by the excavation of the site in 1950, the results of which did not agree with much of his narrative of the history of Somanātha. The reconstruction through archaeology and architectural history indicated an original temple of the ninth or tenth century, with some signs of desecration, but with as much weathering through sea-spray.[54] An eleventh century temple was rebuilt on an earlier plan and this structure was replaced with a more elaborate structure in about the twelfth century. There is little evidence of later structures or reconstructions. This evidence incidentally runs parallel to the Sanskrit inscriptions and the Jaina sources.

On the rebuilding of the temple in 1951, Munshi, by then a minister of the central government suggested that this was an enterprise supported by the Government of India. Jawaharlal Nehru and some of his colleagues objected strongly to the association of the Government of India with this project. They insisted on its being restored as a private venture and to this effect a private Somnath Trust was established to finance and supervise the rebuilding.[55] This

---

53 *British Paramountcy and Indian Renaissance,* History and Culture of the Indian People, Vol. VIII, Part II, 1965, Bombay, 478.

54 B. K.Thapar, "The Temple of Somanātha: History by Exacavation," in Munshi, op.cit, Part III, 71 -90. Bombay, 1951. The sculptures can be seen in the Museum nearby.

55 S. Gopal (ed.), 1994, *Selected Works of Jawaharlal Nehru,* Vol. 16, Part I, Delhi, 270 ff.

introduces a further dimension to the reading of the event, involving the secular credentials of society and state.

The temple of Somanātha was to surface again four decades later as an important political symbol. The theories of the colonial historians, endorsed and garnished by religious nationalism, had now been internalized by various religious nationalisms and more particularly by the ideologies of Hindu and Muslim communalism. Somanātha was being projected as the symbol of Hindu-Muslim antagonism. When the mobilization of Hindus around the Ramjanmabhoomi movement was initiated, the *ratha-yatra* was started from Somanātha and travelled to Ayodhya. Here the subsequent destruction of the Babri Masjid in 1992, was acclaimed by those who endorsed the antagonism as avenging the raid of Maḥmūd on Somanātha.

We may well ask how and when did this dichotomy seen as emerging from the raid, crystallize? Did this happen through modern historians reading too literally from just one set of narratives, without juxtaposing these with other narratives in order to understand the nature of the events? If narratives are read without being placed in the context of their times and the ideologies that might have motivated them, the reading is incomplete and, therefore, distorted. There is also the need to investigate the purpose for which particular texts are written and what bearing this had on the way an event was presented: whether it was ignored or else its importance was exaggerated.

We continue to see such situations as a binary projection of Hindu and Muslim. Yet what should be evident from the sources discussed here, is that there are multiple groups with varying agendas, involved in the way in which events at Somanātha are represented. Thus, there are differentiations in the attitudes of the Persian chronicles towards the Arabs and the Turks. The hostility between the Bohras and the Turks, technically both Muslims, was also part of this confrontation. Biographies and histories from Jaina authors, discussing matters pertinent to the royal court and to the religion of the elite, focus on competing rivalry between the Jainas and the Śaivas. But the sources which focus on a different social group, that of Jaina merchants, seem to be conciliatory towards the confrontation with the Turks, probably because the trading community would have suffered disruptions in periods of raids and campaigns.

From the thirteenth century inscription of Nur-ud-din Firoz, the ship owner from Persia, it seems evident that co-operation in the building of the mosque came from a range of social groups, from the most orthodox priests to those wielding secular authority and from the highest property owners to those with lesser property. These relationships were not determined by the general category of what have been termed "Hindu" and "Muslim" interests and concerns. They varied in accordance with more particular interests, and these drew on identities of ethnicity, economic concerns, religious sectarianism and social status. To narrow these identities to merely the single one of religion – either Hindu or Muslim – is an injustice to their history.

In the retelling of an event, there may be a claim that it encapsulates memory, or a succession of memories. Memory is sometimes claimed in order to create an identity and history based on such claims is used to legitimize the identity. Exploring a fuller understanding of the event is crucial to assessing the validity of this process. That such attempts are often politically motivated becomes evident when one realizes that today the destruction of temples by Muslim rulers is constantly re-iterated, but little mention is made of the destruction of temples by Hindu rulers. The latter were not nearly as many in number but the reasons for their destruction remain significant. It has been argued that temple destruction by Hindu rulers was symbolic of conquest, irrespective of the religion of the conqueror or the defeated. In the case of Muslim rulers, religious iconoclasm was an added reason, except that even here, not all temples were indiscriminately destroyed and the choice of the temple that was destroyed had much to do with political and territorial ambitions.[56]

The claim to historical memory emerges from what has been constructed at a particular point in time and for a particular function, as was done in this case by the British for reasons of colonial politics. That the British were successful in their political intention is proved by Somanātha having now become an icon of antagonism between Hindus and Muslims.

I have tried to show how each set of narratives turn the focus of what Somanātha symbolises: the occasion for the projection of the iconoclast and champion of Islam; the assertion of the superiority of Jainism over Śaivism; the centrality of the profits of trade subordinating other considerations; colonial perceptions of Indian society as having always been an antagonistic duality of Hindu and Muslim; religious nationalism – both Hindu and Muslim – projecting a particular view of the past opposed to a more rational historical enquiry; Hindu nationalism contesting the contemporary secularization of Indian society. But these are not discrete foci. They do require that the understanding of an event should be historically contextual, multi-faceted and aware of the ideological structures implicit in the narratives.

56 R. Eaton, "Temple Destruction and Indo-Muslim States" in this volume.

TEMPLE DESECRATION AND INDO-MUSLIM STATES[1]

RICHARD M. EATON

Framing the Issue

In recent years, especially in the wake of the destruction of the Baburi Mosque in 1992, much public discussion has arisen over the political status of South Asian temples and mosques, and in particular the issue of temples desecrated or replaced by mosques in the pre-British period. While Hindu nationalists have endeavored to document a pattern of wholesale temple destruction by Muslims in this period,[1] few professional historians have engaged the issue, even though it is a properly historical one. This essay aims to examine the evidence of temple desecration with a view to asking: Which temples were desecrated in India's premodern history? When, and by whom? How, and for what purpose? And above all, what might any of this say about the relationship between religion and politics in premodern India? This is a timely topic, since many in India today are looking to the past to justify or condemn public policy with respect to religious monuments.

---

1 This article was originally published in David Gilmartin and Bruce B. Lawrence, eds., *Beyond Turk and Hindu: Rethinking Religious Identities in Islamicate South Asia* (Gainesville: University Press of Florida, 2000).

Much of the contemporary evidence on temple desecration cited by Hindu nationalists is found in Persian material translated and published during the rise of British hegemony in India. Especially influential has been the eight-volume *History of India as Told by Its Own Historians*, first published in 1849 and edited by Sir Henry M. Elliot, who oversaw the bulk of the translations, with the help of John Dowson. But Elliot, keen to contrast what he understood as the justice and efficiency of British rule with the cruelty and despotism of the Muslim rulers who had preceded that rule, was anything but sympathetic to the "Muhammadan" period of Indian history. As he wrote in the book's original preface:

> The common people must have been plunged into the lowest depths of wretchedness and despondency. The few glimpses we have, even among the short Extracts in this single volume, of Hindus slain for disputing with Muhammadans, of general prohibitions against processions, worship, and ablutions, and of other intolerant measures, of idols mutilated, of temples razed, of forcible conversions and marriages, of proscriptions and confiscations, of murders and massacres, and of the sensuality and drunkenness of the tyrants who enjoined them, show us that this picture is not overcharged.[2]

With the advent of British power, on the other hand, "a more stirring and eventful era of India's History commences . . . when the full light of European truth and discernment begins to shed its beams upon the obscurity of the past."[3] Noting the far greater benefits that Englishmen had brought to Indians in a mere half century than Muslims had brought in five centuries, Elliot expressed the hope that his published translations would "make our native subjects more sensible of the immense advantages accruing to them under the mildness and the equity of our rule."[4] Elliot's motives for delegitimizing the Indo-Muslim rulers who had preceded English rule are thus quite clear. Writing on the pernicious influence that this understanding of premodern Indian history had on subsequent generations, the eminent historian Mohammad Habib once remarked, "The peaceful Indian Mussalman, descended beyond doubt from Hindu ancestors, was dressed up in the garb of a foreign barbarian, as a breaker of temples, and an eater of beef, and declared to be a military colonist in the land where he had lived for about thirty or forty centuries. . . . The result of it is seen in the communalistic atmosphere of India today."[5] Although penned many years ago, these words are especially relevant in the context of current controversies over the history of temple desecration in India. For it has been through a selective use of Elliot and Dowson's selective translations of premodern Persian chronicles, together with a selective use of epigraphic data, that Hindu nationalists have sought to find the sort of irrefutable evidence—one of Sita Ram Goel's chapters is entitled "From the Horse's Mouth"—that would demonstrate a persistent pattern of villainy and fanaticism on the part of premodern Indo-Muslim conquerors and rulers.

In reality, though, each scrap of evidence in the matter requires careful scrutiny. Consider an inscription dated 1455 and found over the doorway of a tomb-shrine in Dhar, Madhya Pradesh, formerly the capital of Malwa. The inscription, a Persian *ghazal* of forty-two verses, mentions the destruction of a Hindu temple by one 'Abdullah Shah Changal during the reign of Raja Bhoja, a renowned Paramara king who ruled over the region from 1010 to 1053. In *Hindu Temples: What Happened to Them?* Goel accepts the inscription's reference to temple destruction more or less at face value, as though it were a contemporary newspaper account reporting an objective fact.[6] Unlike Goel, however, the text is concerned not with documenting an instance of temple destruction but with narrating and celebrating the fabulous career of 'Abdullah Shah Changal, the saint who is buried at Dhar. A reading of a larger body of the text reveals, in fact, a complex historiographical process at work:

> This centre became Muhammadan first by him [i.e., 'Abdullah Shah Changal], (and) all the banners of religion were spread. (I have heard) that a few persons had arrived before him at this desolate and ruined place. When the muazzin raised the morning cry like the trumpet-call for the intoxicated *sufis*, the infidels (made an attack from) every wall (?) and each of them rushed with the sword and knife. At last they (the

> infidels) wounded those men of religion, and after killing them concealed (them) in a well. Now this (burial place and) grave of martyrs remained a trace of those holy and pious people.
>
> When the time came that the sun of Reality should shine in this dark and gloomy night, this lion-man ['Abdullah Shah Changal] came from the centre of religion to this old temple with a large force. He broke the images of the false deities, and turned the idol-temple into a mosque. When Rai Bhoj saw this, through wisdom he embraced Islam with the family of all brave warriors. This quarter became illuminated by the light of the Muhammadan law, and the customs of the infidels became obsolete and abolished.
>
> Now this tomb since those old days has been the famous pilgrimage-place of a world. Graves from their oldness became leveled (to the ground), (and) there remained no mount on any grave. There was also (no place) for retirement, wherein the distressed *darvish* could take rest. Thereupon the king of the world gave the order that this top of Tur [Mount Sinai] be built anew. The king of happy countenance, the Sultan of horizons (i.e., the world), the visitors of whose courts are Khaqan (the emperor of Turkistan) and Faghfur (the emperor of China), 'Ala-ud-din Wad-dunya Abu'l-Muzaffar, who is triumphant over his enemies by the grace of God, the Khilji king Mahmud Shah, who is such that by his justice the world has become adorned like paradise, he built afresh this old structure, and this house with its enclosure again became new.[7]

The narrative divides a remembered past into three distinct moments. The first is the period before the arrival of the Hero, 'Abdullah Shah Changal. At this time a small community of Muslims in Malwa, with but a tenuous foothold in the region, were martyred by local non-Muslims, their bodies thrown into a well. The narrative's second moment is the period of the Hero, who comes from the "centre of religion" (Mecca?), smashes images, transforms the temple into a mosque, and converts to Islam the most famous king of the Paramara dynasty— deeds that collectively avenge the martyred Sufis and (re)establish Islam in the region. The narrative's third moment is the period after the Hero's lifetime when his grave, although a renowned place of pilgrimage, has suffered from neglect. Now enters the narrative's other hero, Sultan Mahmud Khalaji, the "king of the world" and "of happy countenance," to whose court the emperors of China and Central Asia pay respect, and by whose justice the world has become adorned like paradise. His great act was to patronize the cult of 'Abdullah Shah by (re)building his shrine, which we are told at text's end included a strong vault, a mosque, and a caravanserai. The inscription closes by offering a prayer that the soul of the benevolent sultan may last until Judgment Day and that his empire may last in perpetuity.

Although Indo-Muslim epigraphs are typically recorded soon after the events they describe, the present one is hardly contemporary, as it was composed some four hundred years after the events to which it refers. Far from being a factual account of a contemporary incident, then, the text presents a richly textured legend elaborated over many generations of oral transmission until 1455, when the story of 'Abdullah Shah Changal and his deeds in Malwa became frozen in the written word that we have before us. As such, the narrative reveals a process by which a particular community at a particular time and place—Muslims in mid-fifteenth-century Malwa—constructed their origins. Central to the story are themes of conversion, martyrdom, redemption, and the patronage of sacred sites by Indo-Muslim royalty, as well as, of course, the destruction of a temple. Whether or not any temple was actually destroyed four hundred years before this narrative was committed to writing, we cannot know with certainty. However, it would seem no more likely that such a desecration had actually occurred than that the renowned Raja Bhoja had been converted to Islam, which the text also claims.

In any event, it is clear that by the mid-fifteenth century the memory of the destruction of a temple, projected into a distant past, had become one among several elements integral to how Muslims in Malwa—or at least those who patronized the composition of this *ghazal*—had come to understand their origins. The case thus suggests that caution is necessary in interpreting claims made in Indo-Muslim literary sources to instances of temple desecration. It also illustrates the central role that temple desecration played in the remembered past of an Indo-Muslim state or community.

Early Instances of Temple Desecration

It is well known that, during the two centuries before 1192, which was when an indigenous Indo-Muslim state and community first appeared in North India, Persianized Turks systematically raided and looted major urban centers of North India, hauling immense loads of movable property to power bases in eastern Afghanistan.[8] The pattern commenced in 986, when the Ghaznavid sultan, Sabuktigin (r. 977-997), attacked and defeated the Hindu Shahi raja who controlled the region between Kabul and northwest Punjab. According to Abu Nasr 'Utbi, the personal secretary to the sultan's son, Sabuktigin "marched out towards Lamghan [located to the immediate east of Kabul], which is a city celebrated for its great strength and abounding in wealth. He conquered it and set fire to the places in its vicinity which were inhabited by infidels, and demolishing the idol-temples, he established Islam in them."[9] Linking religious conversion with military conquest—with conquest serving to facilitate conversion, and conversion to legitimize conquest—'Utbi's brief notice established a rhetorical trope that many subsequent Indo-Muslim chroniclers would repeat, as for example in the case of the 1455 inscription at Dhar, just discussed.

Notwithstanding 'Utbi's religious rhetoric, however, subsequent invasions by Sabuktigin and his more famous son, Mahmud of Ghazni (r. 998-1030), appear to have been undertaken for purely material reasons. Based in Afghanistan and never seeking permanent dominion in India, the earlier Ghaznavid rulers raided and looted Indian cities, including their richly endowed temples loaded with movable wealth, with a view to financing their larger political objectives far to the west in Khurasan.[10] The predatory nature of these raids was also structurally integral to the Ghaznavid political economy: their army was a permanent, professional one built around an elite core of mounted archers who, as slaves, were purchased, equipped, and paid with cash derived from regular infusions of war booty taken alike from Indian and Iranian cities.[11] From the mid-eleventh century, however, Mahmud's successors, cut off from their sources of military manpower in Central Asia first by the Seljuqs and then by the Ghurids, became progressively more provincial, their kingdom focused around their capital of Ghazni in eastern Afghanistan with extensions into the Punjab. And, while the later Ghaznavids continued the predatory raids of the Indian interior for booty, these appear to have been less destructive and more sporadic than those of Sabuktigin and Mahmud.[12]

The dynamics of North Indian politics changed dramatically, however, when the Ghurids, a dynasty of Tajik (eastern Iranian) origins, arrived from central Afghanistan toward the end of the twelfth century. Sweeping aside the Ghaznavids, Ghurid conquerors and their Turkish slave generals ushered in a new sort of state quite unlike that of the foreign-based Ghaznavids. Aspiring to imperial dominion over the whole of North India from a base in the middle of the Indo-Gangetic plain, the new Delhi Sultanate signaled the first attempt to build an indigenous Indo-Muslim state and society in North India. With respect to religious policy, we can identify two principal components to this project: (a) state patronage of an India-based Sufi order, and (b) a policy of selective temple desecration that aimed not, as earlier, to finance the military machine of a vast and distant empire but to delegitimize and extirpate defeated Indian ruling houses. Let us consider these in turn.

Sufism and State Building

"The world is bound up closely with that of the men of faith," wrote the Bahmani court poet 'Abd al-Malik 'Isami in 1350. "In every country, there is a man of piety who keeps it going and well. Although there might be a monarch in every country, yet it is actually under the protection of a fakir [Sufi shaikh]."[13] Here we find a concise statement of the medieval Perso-Islamic conception of how religion and politics interrelate. In 'Isami's view, what had saved the Delhi Sultanate from Mongol conquest was the respect showed by Sultan Muhammad bin Tughluq (r. 1325-51) for the memory of the founder of the Chishti order in India, Shaikh Mu'in al-Din Chishti (d. 1236), to whose tomb in Ajmer the sultan had made a pilgrimage just after engaging with a Mongol army.[14] 'Isami also felt, however, that the decline of Delhi, and of the Tughluq empire generally, had resulted in large part from the demise in 1325 of Nizam al-Din Auliya, Delhi's most renowned shaikh. Conversely, he considered that the arrival in the Deccan of one of Nizam al-Din Auliya's leading spiritual successors, Burhan al-Din Gharib (d. 1337), was the cause of that region's flourishing state at mid-century.[15]

Among all South Asian Sufi orders, the Chishtis were the most closely identified with the political fortunes of Indo-Muslim states, and especially with the planting of such states in parts of South Asia never previously touched by Islamic rule. The pattern began in the first several decades of the fourteenth century, when the order's rise to prominence among Delhi's urban populace coincided with that of the imperial Tughluqs. The two principal Persian poets in India of that time, Amir Hasan and Amir Khusrau, and the leading historian, Zia al-Din Barani, were all disciples of Nizam al-Din Auliya. As writers whose works were widely read, these men were in effect publicists for Nizam al-Din and his order. And since the three were also patronized by the Tughluq court, the public and the ruling classes alike gradually came to associate dynastic fortune with that of the Chishti order.[16] Moreover, as the spiritual power of a charismatic Sufi was believed to adhere to his tomb, shrines at such tombs were patronized by Indo-Muslim rulers just as they were frequented by Muslim devotees. And since the tomb-shrines of the greatest shaikhs of this order were located within South Asia, and not in distant Central Asia or the Middle East as was the case with those of other orders, a ruling dynasty's patronage of Chishti shrines could bolster its claims to being both legitimately Islamic and authentically Indian.

Thus Chishti shaikhs repeatedly participated in the launching of new Indo-Muslim states. At the core of 'Isami's narrative of the Bahmani Revolution, which in 1347 successfully threw off Tughluq overlordship and launched an independent Indo-Muslim state in the Deccan, is a narrative of the passing of the Prophet Muhammad's own mantle (*khirqa*) from Abu Bakr, the first caliph, down to Burhan al-Din Gharib's leading disciple, Zain al-Din Shirazi (d. 1369). It was from that very mantle—"by whose scent one could master both worlds"—that the founder of the Bahmani Sultanate, Sultan Hasan Bahman Shah (r. 1347-58), was said to have received his own power and inspiration.[17] We see the same pattern in Bengal, another former Tughluq province that asserted its independence from Delhi in the mid-fourteenth century. The earliest known monument built by the founder of Bengal's Ilyas Shahi dynasty (1342-1486) was a mosque dedicated in 1342 to Shaikh 'Ala al-Haq (d. 1398), a Sufi shaikh whose own spiritual master was—like Zain al-Din's spiritual master—a disciple of Nizam al-Din Auliya (d. 1325). What is more, the political ascendancy of the Ilyas Shahi dynasty coincided exactly with the spiritual ascendancy of Shaikh 'Ala al-Haq and his own family. Down to the year 1532, fully fourteen successive sultans of Bengal enlisted themselves as disciples of the descendants of this shaikh, while the tomb-shrine of 'Ala al-Haq's own son and successor, Nur Qutb-i 'Alam, became in effect a state shrine to which subsequent sultans made annual pilgrimages.[18]

In short, within the space of just five years, between 1342 and 1347, founders of independent Indo-Muslim dynasties in both Bengal and the Deccan patronized local Chishti shaikhs whose own spiritual masters had migrated from Delhi, where they had studied with the imperial capital's preeminent Sufi shaikh, Nizam al-Din Auliya. The pattern was repeated elsewhere, as the Tughluq empire continued to crumble, giving rise to more provincial successor-states. In 1396, the Tughluq governor of Gujarat, Muzaffar Khan, proclaimed his independence immediately after marching to Ajmer, where he paid his devotions to the tomb of Mu'in al-Din Chishti, the "mother-shrine" of the Chishti order in India.[19] In 1404, soon after proclaiming his own independence from Delhi, the former Tughluq governor of Malwa, Dilawar Khan, described himself as "the disciple of the head of the holy order of Nasir Din Mahmud."[20] The reference here was to Nizam al-Din Auliya's most eminent disciple to have remained in Delhi—Shaikh Nasir al-Din Mahmud (d. 1356), over whose grave Sultan Firuz Shah Tughluq (r. 1351-88) had raised a magnificent tomb several decades earlier.[21]

Nor did the pattern cease with the launching of Tughluq successor states. On entering Delhi in 1526, Babur prayed at the shrine of India's second great Chishti shaikh, Bakhtiyar Kaki (d. 1235), and the new emperor's brother-in-law rebuilt the tomb of Nizam al-Din Auliya. In 1571 Akbar built a tomb for his father, Humayun, near Nizam al-Din's shrine and in the same year began building his new capital of Fatehpur Sikri at the hospice-site of Salim Chishti, the shaikh who had predicted the birth of the emperor's son. Toward the end of his life, this same shaikh tied his turban on the head of that son, the future Jahangir, and pronounced him his spiritual successor. As emperor himself, Jahangir built gates and other buildings at or near the foundational Chishti shrine at Ajmer, as did Shah Jahan as part of his victory celebrations after defeating the raja of Mewar. That emperor's daughter, Jahan Ara, even wrote a biography of Mu'in al-Din Chishti. Shah Jahan's son and successor, Aurangzeb, who sought to build another pan-Indian empire on the Tughluq model, visited and made sizable contributions to Chishti tombs in former Tughluq provinces such as at Gulbarga or Khuldabad, in addition to tombs in Ajmer and Delhi. Even the later Mughals patronized those Chishti shrines to which they still had access in their dwindling domains, as when 'Alamgir II repaired and made additions to the tomb of Nizam al-Din Auliya. Bringing the pattern full circle, the last Mughal emperor, Bahadur Shah II (deposed 1858), built his own mansion adjacent to the shrine of Bakhtiyar Kaki, the very site where Babur had prayed more than three centuries earlier.[22]

In sum, rulers of the entire Mughal dynasty, believing that the blessings of Chishti shaikhs underpinned their worldly success, vigorously patronized the order. Two of Akbar's fourteen pilgrimages to the shrine of Mu'in al-Din Chishti at Ajmer, those of 1568 and 1574, were made immediately after conquering Chittor and Bengal, respectively.[23] Discussing his military successes with the historian 'Abd al-Qadir Badauni, Akbar remarked, "All this (success) has been brought through the Pir [Mu'in al-Din]."[24] Vividly dramatized by Akbar's pilgrimages from Agra to Ajmer, several of them made by foot, the Mughal-Chishti partnership even survived the collapse of the Mughal state. In a sense it persists to this day. The ceremonies, the terminology, and the protocol still found at Chishti shrines generally, and at the Ajmer shrine particularly, reflect the extraordinary intrusion of Mughal courtly culture into that of the Chishti order.[25]

Temple Desecration and State Building

By effectively injecting a legitimizing "substance" into a new body politic, royal patronage of Chishti shaikhs contributed positively to the process of Indo-Muslim state building. Equally important to this process was its negative counterpart: the sweeping away of all prior political authority in newly conquered and annexed territories. When such authority was vested in a ruler whose own legitimacy was associated with a royal temple—typically one that housed an image of a ruling dynasty's state deity, or *raṣṭra-devatā* (usually Vishnu or Śiva)— that temple was normally desecrated, redefined, or destroyed, any of which would have had the effect of detaching a defeated raja from the most prominent manifestation of his former legitimacy. Temples that were not so identified, or temples formerly so identified but abandoned by their royal patrons and thereby rendered politically irrelevant, were normally left unharmed. Such was the case, for example, with the famous temples at Khajuraho south of the Middle Gangetic Plain, which appear to have been abandoned by their Candella royal patrons before Turkish armies reached the area in the early thirteenth century.[26]

It would be wrong to explain this phenomenon by appealing to an essentialized "theology of iconoclasm" felt to be intrinsic to the Islamic religion. While it is true that contemporary Persian sources routinely condemned idolatry (*but-parastī*) on religious grounds, it is also true that attacks on images patronized by enemy kings had been, from about the sixth century A.D. on, thoroughly integrated into Indian political behavior. With their lushly sculpted imagery vividly displaying the mutual interdependence of kings and gods and the co-mingling of divine and human kingship, royal temple complexes of the early medieval period were thoroughly and preeminently political institutions. It was here that, after the sixth century, human kingship was established, contested, and revitalized.[27] Above all, the central icon housed in a royal temple's "womb-chamber" and inhabited by the state deity of the temple's royal patron expressed the shared sovereignty of king and deity. Moreover, notwithstanding that temple priests endowed a royal temple's deity with attributes of transcendent and universal power, that same deity was also understood as having a very special relationship, indeed a sovereign relationship, with the particular geographical site in which its temple complex was located.[28] As revealed in temple narratives, even the physical removal of an image from its original site could not break the link between deity and geography.[29] The bonding between king, god, temple, and land in early medieval India is well illustrated in a passage from *Bṛhatsaṃhitā*, a text from the sixth century A.D.: "If a Śiva linga, image, or temple breaks apart, moves, sweats, cries, speaks, or otherwise acts with no apparent cause, this warns of the destruction of the king and his territory."[30] In short, from about the sixth century on, images and temples associated with dynastic authority were considered politically vulnerable.

Given these perceived connections between temples, images, and their royal patrons, it is hardly surprising that early medieval Indian history abounds in instances of temple desecration that occurred amidst interdynastic conflicts. In A.D. 642, according to local tradition, the Pallava king, Narasimhavarman I, looted the image of Ganesha from the Chalukyan capital of Vatapi. Fifty years later, armies of those same Chalukyas invaded North India and brought back to the Deccan what appear to be images of Ganga and Yamuna, looted from defeated powers there. In the eighth century, Bengali troops sought revenge on King Lalitaditya by destroying what they thought was the image of Vishnu Vaikuntha, the state deity of Lalitaditya's kingdom in Kashmir. In the early ninth century, the Rashtrakuta king, Govinda III, invaded and occupied Kanchipuram, which so intimidated the king of Sri Lanka that he sent Govinda several (probably Buddhist) images representing the Sinhala state. The Rashtrakuta king then installed these in a Śaiva temple in his capital. About the same time the Pandyan king, Srimara Srivallabha, also invaded Sri Lanka and took back to his capital a golden Buddha image—"a synecdoche for the integrity of the Sinhalese polity itself"—that had been installed in the kingdom's jewel palace. In the early tenth century, the Pratihara king, Herambapala, seized a solid gold image of Vishnu Vaikuntha when he defeated the Sahi king of Kangra. A few years later, the same image was seized from the Pratiharas by the Candella king, Yaśovarman, and installed in the Lakshmana temple of Khajuraho. In the early eleventh century, the Chola king, Rajendra I, furnished his capital with images he had seized from several prominent neighboring kings: Durga and Ganesha images from the Chalukyas; Bhairava, Bhairavi, and Kali images from the Kalingas of Orissa; a Nandi image from the Eastern Chalukyas; and a bronze Śiva image from the Palas of Bengal. In the mid-eleventh century, the Chola king, Rajadhiraja, defeated the Chalukyas and plundered Kalyani, taking a large black stone door guardian to his capital in Thanjavur, where it was displayed to his subjects as a trophy of war.[31]

While the dominant pattern here was one of looting royal temples and carrying off images of state deities,[32] we also hear of Hindu kings destroying the royal temples of their political adversaries. In the early tenth century, the Rashtrakuta monarch, Indra III, not only destroyed the temple of Kalapriya (at Kalpa near the Jamuna River), patronized by the Rashtrakutas' deadly enemies, the Pratiharas, but they took special delight in recording the fact.[33]

In short, it is clear that temples had been the natural sites for the contestation of kingly authority well before the coming of Muslim Turks to India. Not surprisingly, Turkish invaders, when attempting to plant their own rule in early medieval India, followed and continued established patterns. Table 1 (pp. 130-33) gives dates and places, which are keyed to three maps (pp. 127-29). These cannot give the complete picture of temple desecration after the establishment of Turkish power in Upper India. Undoubtedly, some temples were desecrated, but the facts were never recorded, or the facts were recorded but the records themselves no longer survive. Conversely, later Indo-Muslim chroniclers, seeking to glorify the religious zeal of earlier Muslim rulers, sometimes attributed acts of temple desecration to such rulers even when no contemporary evidence supports the claims.[34] As a result, we shall never know the precise number of temples desecrated in Indian history. Nonetheless, by relying strictly on evidence found in contemporary or near-contemporary epigraphs and literary evidence spanning more than five centuries (1192–1729), one may identify eighty instances of temple desecration whose historicity appears reasonably certain. Although this figure falls well short of the 60,000 claimed by some Hindu nationalists,[35] a review of these data suggests several broad patterns.

First, acts of temple desecration were almost invariably carried out by military officers or ruling authorities; that is, such acts that we know about were undertaken by the state. Second, the chronology and geography of the data indicate that acts of temple desecration typically occurred on the cutting edge of a moving military frontier. From Ajmer— significantly, also the wellspring of Chishti piety—the post-1192 pattern of temple desecration moved swiftly down the Gangetic Plain as Turkish military forces sought to extirpate local ruling houses in the late twelfth and early thirteenth centuries (see table 1 and map 1: nos. 1-9). In Bihar, this included the targeting of Buddhist monastic establishments at Odantapuri, Vikramasila, and Nalanda. Detached from a Buddhist laity, these establishments had by this time become dependent on the patronage of local royal authorities, with whom they were identified. In the 1230s, Iltutmish carried the Delhi Sultanate's authority into Malwa (nos. 10-11), and by the onset of the fourteenth century the Khalaji sultans had opened up a corridor through eastern Rajasthan into Gujarat (nos. 12-14, 16-17).

Delhi's initial raids on peninsular India, on which the Khalajis embarked between 1295 and the early decades of the fourteenth century (nos. 15, 18-19), appear to have been driven not by a goal of annexation but by the Sultanate's need for wealth with which to defend North India from Mongol attacks.[36] For a short time, then, peninsular India stood in the same relation to the North—namely, as a source of plunder for financing distant military operations—as North India had stood in relation to Afghanistan three centuries earlier, in the days of Mahmud of Ghazni. In 1323, however, a new North Indian dynasty, the Tughluqs, sought permanent dominion in the Deccan, which the future Sultan Muhammad bin Tughluq established by uprooting royally patronized temples in western Andhra (nos. 20-22). Somewhat later Sultan Firuz Tughluq did the same in Orissa (no. 23).

From the late fourteenth century, as the tide of Tughluq imperialism had receded from Gujurat and the Deccan, newly emerging successor states sought to expand their own political frontiers in those areas. This, too, is reflected in instances of temple desecration, as the ex-Tughluq governor of Gujarat and his successors consolidated their authority there (see table 1 and map 2: nos. 25-26, 31-32, 34-35, 38-39, 42), or as the Delhi empire's successors in the south, the Bahmani sultans, challenged Vijayanagara's claims to dominate the Raichur doab and the Tamil coast (nos. 33, 41). The pattern was repeated in Kashmir by Sultan Sikandar (nos. 27-30) and in the mid-fifteenth century when the independent sultanate of Malwa contested renewed Rajput power in eastern Rajasthan after Delhi's authority there had waned (nos. 36-37). In the early sixteenth century, when the Lodi dynasty of Afghans sought to reassert Delhi's sovereignty over neighboring Rajput houses, we again find instances of temple desecration (nos. 43-45). So do we in the later sixteenth and early seventeenth centuries, when the Bahmani kingdom's principal successor states, Bijapur and Golconda, challenged the territorial sovereignty of Orissan kings (nos. 55, 59; maps 2 and 3), of Vijayanagara (no. 47), and of the latter's successor states—especially in the southern Andhra country (nos. 50-51, 53-54, 60-61; maps 2 and 3).

Unlike the Deccan, where Indo-Muslim states had been expanding at the expense of non-Muslim states, in North India the Mughals under Babur, Humayun, and Akbar—that is, between 1526 and 1605—grew mainly at the expense of defeated Afghans. As non-Hindus, the latter had never shared sovereignty with deities patronized in royal temples, which probably explains the absence of firm evidence of temple desecration by any of the early Mughals, in Ayodhya or elsewhere.[37] However, when Mughal armies pushed beyond the frontiers of territories formerly ruled by the Delhi sultans and sought to annex the domains of Hindu rulers, we again find instances of temple desecration. In 1661 the governor of Bengal, Mir Jumla, sacked the temples of the raja of Kuch Bihar, who had been harassing the northern frontiers of Mughal territory (no. 64; map 3). The next year, with a view to annexing Assam to the imperial domain, the governor pushed far up the Brahmaputra Valley and desecrated temples of the Ahom rajas, replacing the principal one at Garhgaon with a mosque (nos. 65-66).

All of these instances of temple desecration occurred in the context of military conflicts when Indo-Muslim states expanded into the domains of non-Muslim rulers. Contemporary chroniclers and inscriptions left by the victors leave no doubt that field commanders, governors, or sultans viewed the desecration of royal temples as a normal means of decoupling a Hindu king's legitimate authority from his former kingdom, and more specifically, of decoupling that former king from the image of the state deity that was publicly understood as protecting the king and his kingdom. This was accomplished in several ways. Most typically, temples considered essential to the constitution of enemy authority were destroyed. Occasionally, temples were converted into mosques, which more visibly conflated the disestablishment of former sovereignty with the establishment of a new one.[38]

The form of desecration that showed the greatest continuity with pre-Turkish practice was the seizure of the image of a defeated king's state deity and its abduction to the victor's capital as a trophy of war. In February 1299, for example, Ulugh Khan sacked Gujarat's famous temple of Somnath and sent its largest image to Sultan 'Ala al-Din Khalaji's court in Delhi (no. 16; map 1). When Firuz Tughluq invaded Orissa in 1359 and learned that the region's most important temple was that of Jagannath located inside the raja's fortress in Puri, he carried off the stone image of the god and installed it in Delhi "in an ignominious position" (no. 23). In 1518, when the court in Delhi came to suspect the loyalty of a tributary Rajput chieftain in Gwalior, Sultan Ibrahim Lodi marched to the famous fortress, stormed it, and seized a brass image of Nandi evidently situated adjacent to the chieftain's Śiva temple. Brought back to Delhi, it was installed in the city's Baghdad Gate (no. 46; map 2). Similarly, in 1579, when Golconda's army, led by Murahari Rao, was campaigning south of the Krishna River, Rao annexed the entire region to Qutb Shahi domains and sacked the popular Ahobilam temple, whose ruby-studded image he brought back to Golconda and presented to his sultan as a war trophy (no. 51). Although the Ahobilam temple had only local appeal, it had close associations with prior sovereign authority, since it had been patronized and even visited by the powerful and most famous king of Vijayanagara, Krishna Deva Raya.[39]

In each of these instances, the deity's image, taken as war trophy to the capital city of the victorious sultan, was radically detached from its former context and transformed from a living to a dead image. However, sacked images were not invariably abducted to the victor's capital. In 1556, the Gajapati raja of Orissa had entered into a pact with the Mughal emperor, Akbar, the distant adversary of the sultan of Bengal, Sulaiman Karrani. The raja had also given refuge to Sulaiman's more proximate adversary, Ibrahim Sur, and offered to assist the latter in his ambitions to conquer Bengal and overthrow the Karrani dynasty. As Sulaiman could hardly have tolerated such threats to his stability, he sent an army into Orissa that went straight to the Gajapati kingdom's state temple of Jagannath and looted its images. But here the goal was not annexation but only punishment, which might explain why the Gajapati state images were not carried back to the Bengali capital as trophies of war.[40]

Whatever form they took, acts of temple desecration were never directed at the people but at the enemy king and the image that incarnated and displayed his state deity. A contemporary description of a 1661 Mughal campaign in Kuch Bihar, which resulted in the annexation of the region, makes it clear that Mughal authorities were guided by two principal concerns. The first was to destroy the image of the state deity of the defeated raja, Bhim Narayan. And the second was to prevent Mughal troops from looting or in any way harming the general population of Kuch Bihar. To this end, we are informed that the chief judge of Mughal Bengal, Saiyid Muhammad Sadiq,

> was directed to issue prohibitory orders that nobody was to touch the cash and property of the people, and he should go personally and establish order everywhere. He was asked to confiscate the treasure of Bhim Narayan, break the idols and introduce the laws of Islam. Sayyid Sadiq issued strict prohibitory orders so that nobody had the courage to break the laws or to plunder the property of the inhabitants. The punishment for disobeying the order was that the hands, ears or noses of the plunderers were cut. Sayyid Sadiq busied himself in giving protection to the life and property of the subjects and the destitutes.[41]

In newly annexed areas formerly ruled by non-Muslims, as in the case of Kuch Bihar, Mughal officers took appropriate measures to secure the support of the common people, who after all created the material wealth upon which the entire imperial edifice rested.

Temple Protection and State Maintenance

If the idea of conquest became manifest in the destruction of those temples associated with former enemies, what happened once the land and the subjects of those former states became successfully integrated into an Indo-Muslim state? On this point, the data are quite clear: pragmatism as well as time-honored traditions of both Islamic and Indian statecraft dictated that temples lying within such states be left unmolested. We learn from a Sanskrit inscription, for example, that in 1326, thirteen years after the northern Deccan had been annexed to the Tughluq empire, Sultan Muhammad bin Tughluq appointed Muslim officials to repair a Śiva temple in Kalyana (in Bidar District), thereby facilitating the resumption of normal worship that had been disrupted by local disturbances.[42] According to that sultan's interpretation of Islamic law, anybody who paid the poll tax (*jizya*) could build temples in territories ruled by Muslims.[43]

Such views continued to hold sway until modern times. Within several decades of Muhammad bin Tughluq's death, Sultan Shihab al-Din (1355-73) of Kashmir rebuked his Brahman minister for having suggested melting down Hindu and Buddhist images in his kingdom as a means of obtaining quick cash. In elaborating his ideas on royal patronage of religion, the sultan referred to the deeds of figures drawn from classical Hindu mythology. "Some [kings]," he said,

> have obtained renown by setting up images of gods, others by worshiping them, some by duly maintaining them. And some, by demolishing them! How great is the enormity of such a deed! Sagara became famous by creating the sea and the rivers. . . . Bhagiratha obtained fame by bringing down the Ganges. Jealous of Indra's fame, Dushyanata acquired renown by conquering the world; and Rama by killing Ravana when the latter

> had purloined Sita. King Shahvadina [Shihab al-Din], it will be said, plundered the image of a god; and this fact, dreadful as Yama [death], will make the men in future tremble.[44]

About a century later, Muslim jurists advised the future Sikandar Lodi of Delhi (r. 1489-1517) that "it is not lawful to lay waste ancient idol temples, and it does not rest with you to prohibit ablution in a reservoir which has been customary from ancient times."[45]

The pattern of post-conquest temple protection, and even patronage, is especially clear when we come to the imperial Mughals, whose overall views on the subject are captured in official pronouncements on Sultan Mahmud of Ghazni, one of the most controversial figures in Indian history. It is well known that in the early eleventh century, before the establishment of Indo-Muslim rule in North India, the Ghaznavid sultan had made numerous, and very destructive, attacks on the region. Starting with the writings of his own contemporary and court poet, Firdausi (d. 1020), Mahmud's career soon became legend, as generations of Persian poets lionized Mahmud as a paragon of Islamic kingly virtue, celebrating his infamous attacks on Indian temples as models for what other pious sultans should do.[46] But the Ghaznavid sultan never undertook the responsibility of actually governing any part of the subcontinent whose temples he so wantonly plundered. Herein lies the principal difference between the careers of Mahmud and Abu'l-Fazl, Akbar's chief minister and the principal architect of Mughal imperial ideology. Reflecting the sober values that normally accompany the practice of governing large, multi-ethnic states, Abu'l-Fazl attributed Mahmud's excesses to fanatical bigots who, having incorrectly represented India as "a country of unbelievers at war with Islam," incited the sultan's unsuspecting nature, which led to "the wreck of honour and the shedding of blood and the plunder of the virtuous."[47]

Indeed, from Akbar's time (r. 1556-1605) forward, Mughal rulers treated temples lying within their sovereign domain as state property; accordingly, they undertook to protect both the physical structures and their Brahman functionaries. At the same time, by appropriating Hindu religious institutions to serve imperial ends—a process involving complex overlappings of political and religious codes of power—the Mughals became deeply implicated in institutionalized Indian religions, in dramatic contrast to their British successors, who professed a hands-off policy in this respect. Thus we find Akbar allowing high-ranking Rajput officers in his service to build their own monumental temples in the provinces to which they were posted.[48] His successors went further. Between 1590 and 1735, Mughal officials repeatedly oversaw, and on occasion even initiated, the renewal of Orissa's state cult, that of Jagannath in Puri. By sitting on a canopied chariot while accompanying the cult's annual car festival, Shah Jahan's officials ritually demonstrated that it was the Mughal emperor, operating through his appointed officers (*manṣabdār*), who was the temple's—and hence the god's—ultimate lord and protector.[49] Such actions in effect projected a hierarchy of hybridized political and religious power that descended from the Mughal emperor to his *manṣabdār*, from the *manṣabdār* to the god Jagannath and his temple, from Jagannath to the sub-imperial king who patronized the god, and from the king to his subjects. For the Mughals, politics within their sovereign domains never meant annihilating prior authority. It meant appropriating authority within a hierarchy of power that flowed from the Peacock Throne to the mass of commoners below.

Such ideas continued into the reign of Aurangzeb (1658-1707), whose orders to local officials in Benares in 1659 clearly indicate that Brahman temple functionaries there, together with the temples at which they officiated, merited state protection:

> In these days information has reached our court that several people have, out of spite and rancor, harassed the Hindu residents of Benares and nearby places, including a group of Brahmans who are in charge of ancient temples there. These people want to remove those Brahmans from their charge of temple-keeping, which has caused them considerable distress. Therefore, upon receiving this order, you must see that nobody

> unlawfully disturbs the Brahmans or other Hindus of that region, so that they might remain in their traditional place and pray for the continuance of the Empire.[50]

By way of justifying this order, the emperor noted, "According to the Holy Law and the exalted creed, it has been established that ancient temples should not be torn down." On this point, Aurangzeb aligned himself with the theory and practice of Indo-Muslim ruling precedent. But then he added, "Nor should new temples be built"—a view that broke decisively from Akbar's policy of permitting his Rajput officers to build their own temple complexes in Mughal territory.[51] Although this order appears to have applied only to Benares—many new temples were built elsewhere in India during Aurangzeb's reign[52]—one might wonder what prompted the emperor's anxiety in this matter.

Temple Desecration and State Maintenance

It seems certain that Indo-Muslim rulers were well aware of the highly charged political and religious relationship between a royal Hindu patron and his client-temple. Hence, even when former rulers or their descendants had been comfortably assimilated into an Indo-Muslim state's ruling class, there always remained the possibility, and hence the occasional suspicion, that a temple's latent political significance might be activated and serve as a power base to further its patron's political aspirations. Such considerations might explain why it was that, when a subordinate non-Muslim officer in an Indo-Muslim state showed signs of disloyalty—and especially if he engaged in open rebellion—the state often desecrated the temple(s) most clearly identified with that officer. After all, if temples lying within its domain were viewed as state property, and if a government officer who was also a temple's patron demonstrated disloyalty to the state, from a juridical standpoint ruling authorities felt justified in treating that temple as an extension of the officer and hence liable for punishment.

Thus in 1478, when the Bahmanis' garrison in Kondapalle mutinied, murdered its governor, and entrusted the fort to Bhimraj Oriyya, who until that point had been a Bahmani client, the sultan personally marched to the site and, after a six-month siege, stormed the fort, destroyed its temple, and built a mosque on the site (no. 40). A similar event occurred in 1659, when Shivaji Bhonsle, the son of a loyal and distinguished officer serving the 'Adil Shahi sultans of Bijapur, seized a government port on the northern Konkan coast, thereby disrupting the flow of external trade to and from the capital. Responding to what it considered an act of treason, the government deputed a high-ranking officer, Afzal Khan, to punish the Maratha rebel. Before marching to confront Shivaji himself, however, the Bijapur general first proceeded to Tuljapur and desecrated a temple dedicated to the goddess Bhavani, to which Shivaji and his family had been personally devoted (no. 63; map 3).

We find the same pattern with the Mughals. In 1613 while at Pushkar, near Ajmer, Jahangir ordered the desecration of an image of Varaha that had been housed in a temple belonging to an uncle of Rana Amar of Mewar, the emperor's arch enemy (see table 1 and map 3: no. 56). In 1635 his son and successor, Shah Jahan, destroyed the great temple at Orchha, which had been patronized by the father of Raja Jajhar Singh, a high-ranking Mughal officer who was at that time in open rebellion against the emperor (no. 58). In 1669, there arose a rebellion in Benares among landholders, some of whom were suspected of having helped Shivaji, who was Aurangzeb's arch enemy, escape from imperial detention. It was also believed that Shivaji's escape had been initially facilitated by Jai Singh, the great-grandson of Raja Man Singh, who almost certainly built Benares's great Vishvanath temple. It was against this background that the emperor ordered the destruction of that temple in September 1669 (no. 69).[53] About the same time, serious Jat rebellions broke out in the area around Mathura, in which the patron of that city's congregational mosque had been killed. So in early 1670, soon after the ringleader of these rebellions had been captured near Mathura, Aurangzeb ordered the destruction of the city's Keshava Deva temple, and he built an Islamic structure (*'īdgāh*) on its site (no. 70).[54] Nine years later, the emperor ordered the destruction of several prominent temples in Rajasthan that had become associated with imperial enemies. These included temples in Khandela patronized by refractory chieftains there, temples in Jodhpur patronized by a former supporter of the emperor's brother and arch rival, and the royal temples in Udaipur and Chitor patronized by Rana Raj Singh after it was learned that that Rajput chieftain had withdrawn his loyalty to the Mughal state (nos. 71-74).

Considerable misunderstanding has arisen from a passage in the *Ma'athir-i 'Alamgiri* concerning an order on the status of Hindu temples that Aurangzeb issued in April 1669, just months before his destruction of the Benares and Mathura temples. The passage has been construed to mean that the emperor ordered the destruction not only of the Vishvanath temple at Benares and the Keshava Deva temple at Mathura but of all temples in the empire.[55] The passage reads as follows: "Orders respecting Islamic affairs were issued to the governors of all the provinces that the schools and places of worship of the irreligious be subject to demolition and that with the utmost urgency the manner of teaching and the public practices of the sects of these misbelievers be suppressed."[56] The order did not state that schools or places of worship be demolished; rather, it said that they were *subject* to demolition, implying that local authorities were required to make investigations before taking action.

More important, the sentence immediately preceding this passage provides the context in which we may find the order's overall intent. On 8 April 1669, Aurangzeb's court received reports that in Thatta, Multan, and especially in Benares, Brahmans in "established schools" *(mudāris-i muqarrar)* had been engaged in teaching false books (*kutub-i bāṭila*) and that both Hindu and Muslim "admirers and students" had been traveling over great distances to study the "ominous sciences" taught by this "deviant group."[57] We do not know what sort of teaching or "false books" were involved here, or why both Muslims and Hindus were attracted to them, although these are intriguing questions. What is clear is that the court was primarily concerned, indeed exclusively concerned, with curbing the influence of a certain mode of teaching (*ṭaur-i dars-o-tadrīs*) within the imperial domain. Far from being, then, a general order for the immediate destruction of all temples in the empire, the order was responding to specific reports of an educational nature and was targeted at investigating those institutions where a certain kind of teaching had been taking place.

In sum, apart from his prohibition on building new temples in Benares, Aurangzeb's policies respecting temples within imperial domains generally followed those of his predecessors. Viewing temples within their domains as state property, Aurangzeb and Indo-Muslim rulers in general punished disloyal Hindu officers in their service by desecrating temples with which they were associated. How, one might then ask, did they punish disloyal Muslim officers? Since officers in all Indo-Muslim states belonged to hierarchically ranked service cadres, infractions short of rebellion normally resulted in demotions in rank, while serious crimes like treason were generally punished by execution, regardless of the perpetrator's religious affiliation.[58]

No evidence, however, suggests that ruling authorities attacked public monuments like mosques or Sufi shrines that had been patronized by disloyal or rebellious officers. Nor were such monuments desecrated when one Indo-Muslim kingdom conquered another and annexed its territories. To the contrary, new rulers were quick to honor and support the shrines of those Chishti shaikhs that had been patronized by those they had defeated. As we have seen, Babur, upon seizing Delhi from the last of the city's ruling sultans, lost no time in patronizing the city's principal Chishti tomb-shrines. The pattern was repeated as the Mughals expanded into the provinces formerly ruled by Muslims. Upon conquering Bengal in 1574, the Mughals showered their most lavish patronage on the two Chishti shrines in Pandua—those of Shaikh 'Ala al-Haq (d. 1398) and Shaikh Nur Qutb-i 'Alam (d. 1459)—which had been the principal object of state patronage by the previous dynasty of Bengal sultans.[59] And when he extended Mughal dominion over defeated Muslim states of the Deccan, the dour Aurangzeb, notwithstanding his reputation for eschewing saint cults, made sizable contributions to those Chishti shrines in Khuldabad and Gulbarga that had helped legitimize earlier Muslim dynasties there.

Temples and Mosques Contrasted

Data presented in the foregoing discussion suggest that mosques or shrines carried very different political meanings than did royal temples in independent Hindu states or temples patronized by Hindu officers serving in Indo-Muslim states. For Indo-Muslim rulers, building mosques was considered an act of royal piety, even a duty. But all actors, rulers and ruled alike, seem to have recognized that the deity worshiped in mosques or shrines had no personal connection with a Muslim monarch. Nor were such monuments thought of as underpinning, far less actually constituting, the authority of an Indo-Muslim king. This point is illustrated in a reported dispute between the emperor Aurangzeb and a Sufi named Shaikh Muhammadi (d. 1696). As a consequence of this dispute, in which the shaikh refused to renounce views that the emperor considered theologically deviant, Shaikh Muhammadi was ordered to leave the imperial domain. When the Sufi instead took refuge in a local mosque, Aurangzeb claimed that this would not do, since the mosque was also within imperial territory. But the shaikh only remarked on the emperor's arrogance, noting that a mosque was the house of God and therefore only His property. The standoff ended with the shaikh's imprisonment in Aurangabad fort—property that was unambiguously imperial.[60]

This incident suggests that mosques in Mughal India, though religiously potent, were considered detached from both land and dynastic authority and hence politically inactive. As such, their desecration could have had no relevance to the business of disestablishing a regime that had patronized them. Not surprisingly, then, when Hindu rulers established their authority over territories of defeated Muslim rulers, they did not as a rule desecrate mosques or shrines, as when Shivaji established a Maratha kingdom on the ashes of Bijapur's former dominions in Maharashtra, or when Vijayanagara annexed the former territories of the Bahmanis or their successors.[61] In fact, the rajas of Vijayanagara, as is well known, built their own mosques, evidently to accommodate the sizable number of Muslims employed in their armed forces.

By contrast, monumental royal temple complexes of the early medieval period were considered politically active, inasmuch as the state deities they housed were understood as expressing the shared sovereignty of king and deity over a particular dynastic realm.[62] Therefore, when Indo-Muslim commanders or rulers looted the consecrated images of defeated opponents and carried them off to their own capitals as war trophies, they were in a sense conforming to customary rules of Indian politics. Similarly, when they destroyed a royal temple or converted it into a mosque, ruling authorities were building on a political logic that they knew placed supreme political significance on such temples. That same significance, in turn, rendered temples just as deserving of peacetime protection as it rendered them vulnerable in times of conflict.

Temple Desecration and the Rhetoric of State Building

Much misunderstanding over the place of temple desecration in Indian history results from a failure to distinguish the rhetoric from the practice of Indo-Muslim state formation. Whereas the former tends to be normative, conservative, and rigidly ideological, the latter tends to be pragmatic, eclectic, and non-ideological. Rhetorically, we know, temple desecration figured very prominently in Indo-Muslim chronicles as a necessary and even meritorious constituent of state formation.[63] In 1350, for example, the poet-chronicler 'Isami gave the following advice to his royal patron, 'Ala al-Din Hasan Bahman Shah, the founder of the Bahmani kingdom in the Deccan: "If you and I, O man of intellect, have a holding in this country and are in a position to replace the idol-houses by mosques and sometimes forcibly to break the Brahmanic thread and enslave women and children—all this is due to the glory of Mahmud [of Ghazni].... The achievements that you make today will also become a story tomorrow."[64] But the new sultan appears to have been more concerned with political stability than with the glorious legacy his court poet would wish him to pursue. There is no evidence that he converted any temples to mosques. After all, by carving out territory from lands formerly lying within the Delhi Sultanate, the founder of the Bahmani state had inherited a domain void of independent Hindu kings and hence void, too, of temples that might have posed a political threat to his fledgling kingdom.

Unlike temple desecration or the patronage of Chishti shaikhs, both of which appear in the contemporary rhetoric on Indo-Muslim state building, a third activity, the use of explicitly Indian political rituals, occupied no place whatsoever in that rhetoric. Here we may consider the way Indo-Muslim rulers used the rich political symbolism of the Ganges River, whose mythic associations with imperial kingship had been well established since Mauryan times (321–181 B.C.). Each in its own way, the mightiest imperial formations of the early medieval peninsula—the Chalukyas, the Rashtrakutas, and the Cholas—claimed to have "brought" the Ganges River down to their southern capitals, seeking thereby to legitimize their claims to imperial sovereignty. Although the Chalukyas and the Rashtrakutas did this symbolically, probably through their insignia, the Cholas literally transported pots of Ganges water to their southern, capital.[65] And, we are told, so did Muhammad bin Tughluq in the years after 1327, when that sultan established Daulatabad, in Maharashtra, as the new co-capital of the Delhi Sultanate's vast, all-India empire.[66] In having Ganges water carried a distance of forty days' journey from North India "for his own personal use," the sultan was conforming to an authentically

Indian imperial ritual. Several centuries later, the Muslim sultans of Bengal, on the occasion of their own coronation ceremonies, would wash themselves with holy water that had been brought to their capital from the ancient holy site of Ganga Sagar, located where the Ganges River emptied into the Bay of Bengal.[67] No Indo-Muslim chronicle or contemporary inscription associates the use of Ganges water with the establishment or maintenance of Indo-Muslim states. We hear this only from foreign visitors: an Arab traveler in the case of Muhammad bin Tughluq, a Portuguese friar in the case of the sultans of Bengal. Similarly, the image of a Mughal official seated in a canopied chariot and presiding over the Jagannath car festival comes to us not from Mughal chronicles but from an English traveler who happened to be in Puri in 1633.[68] Such disjunctures between the rhetoric and the practice of royal sovereignty also appear, of course, with respect to the founding of non-Muslim states. We know, for example, that Brahman ideologues, writing in chaste Sanskrit, spun elaborate tales of how warriors and sages founded the Vijayanagara state by combining forces for a common defense of *dharma* from assaults by barbaric (*mleccha*) Turkic outsiders. This is the Vijayanagara of rhetoric, a familiar story. But the Vijayanagara of practical politics rested on very different foundations, which included the adoption of the titles, the dress, the military organization, the ruling ideology, the architecture, and the political economy of the contemporary Islamicate world.[69] As with Indo-Muslim states, we hear of such practices mainly from outsiders—merchants, diplomats, travelers—and not from Brahman chroniclers and ideologues.

Conclusion

One often hears that between the thirteenth and eighteenth centuries, Indo-Muslim states, driven by a Judeo-Islamic "theology of iconoclasm," by fanaticism, or by sheer lust for plunder, wantonly and indiscriminately indulged in the desecration of Hindu temples. Such a picture cannot, however, be sustained by evidence from original sources for the period after 1192. Had instances of temple desecration been driven by a "theology of iconoclasm," as some have claimed,[70] such a theology would have committed Muslims in India to destroying all temples everywhere, including ordinary village temples, as opposed to the strategically selective operation that seems actually to have taken place. Rather, the original data associate instances of temple desecration with the annexation of newly conquered territories held by enemy kings whose domains lay in the path of moving military frontiers. Temple desecrations also occurred when Hindu patrons of prominent temples committed acts of treason or disloyalty to the Indo-Muslim states they served. Otherwise, temples lying within Indo-Muslim sovereign domains, viewed normally as protected state property, were left unmolested.

Finally, it is important to identify the different meanings that Indians invested in religious monuments and the different ways these monuments were understood to relate to political authority. In the reign of Aurangzeb, Shaikh Muhammadi took refuge in a mosque believing that the structure—being fundamentally apolitical, indeed above politics— lay beyond the Mughal emperor's reach. Contemporary royal temples, on the other hand, were understood as highly charged political monuments, a circumstance that rendered them fatally vulnerable to outside attack. Therefore, by targeting for desecration those temples that were associated with defeated kings, conquering Turks, when they made their own bid for sovereign domain in India, were subscribing to, even while they were exploiting, indigenous notions of royal legitimacy. Contemporary Sanskrit inscriptions never identified Indo-Muslim invaders in terms of their religion, as Muslims, but most generally in terms of their linguistic affiliation (most typically as Turk, "turushka"). That is, they were construed as but one ethnic community in India amidst many others.[71] In the same way, B. D. Chattopadhyaya locates within early medieval Brahmanical discourse an "essential urge to legitimize" any ruling authority so long as it was effective and responsible. This urge was manifested, for example, in the perception of the Tughluqs as legitimate successors to the Tomaras and Cahamanas; of a Muslim ruler of Kashmir as having a lunar, Pandava lineage; or of the Mughal emperors as supporters of Ramarajya (the "kingship of Lord Rama").[72] It is likely that Indo-Muslim policies of protecting temples within their sovereign domains contributed positively to such perceptions.

In sum, by placing known instances of temple desecration in the larger contexts of Indo-Muslim state building and state maintenance, one can find patterns suggesting a rational basis for something commonly dismissed as irrational, or worse. These patterns also suggest points of continuity with Indian practices that had become customary well before the thirteenth century. Such points of continuity in turn call into serious question the sort of civilizational divide between India's "Hindu" and "Muslim" periods first postulated in British colonial historiography and subsequently replicated in both Pakistani and Hindu nationalist schools. Finally, this essay has sought to identify the different meanings that contemporary actors invested in the public monuments they patronized or desecrated, and to reconstruct those meanings on the basis of the practice, and not just the rhetoric, of those actors. It is hoped that the approaches and hypotheses suggested here might facilitate the kind of responsible and constructive discussion that this controversial topic so badly needs.

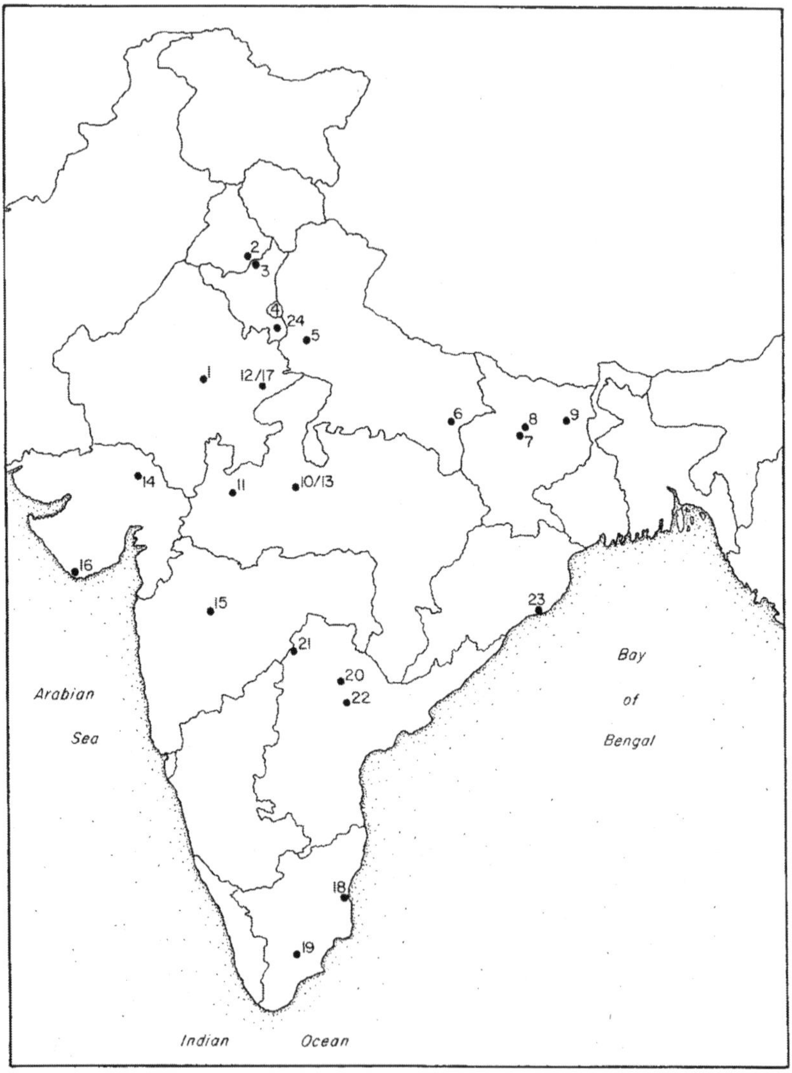

Map 1. Temple Desecrations, 1192–1394: Imperialism of the Delhi Sultanate [Note: Numbers are keyed to the Table.]

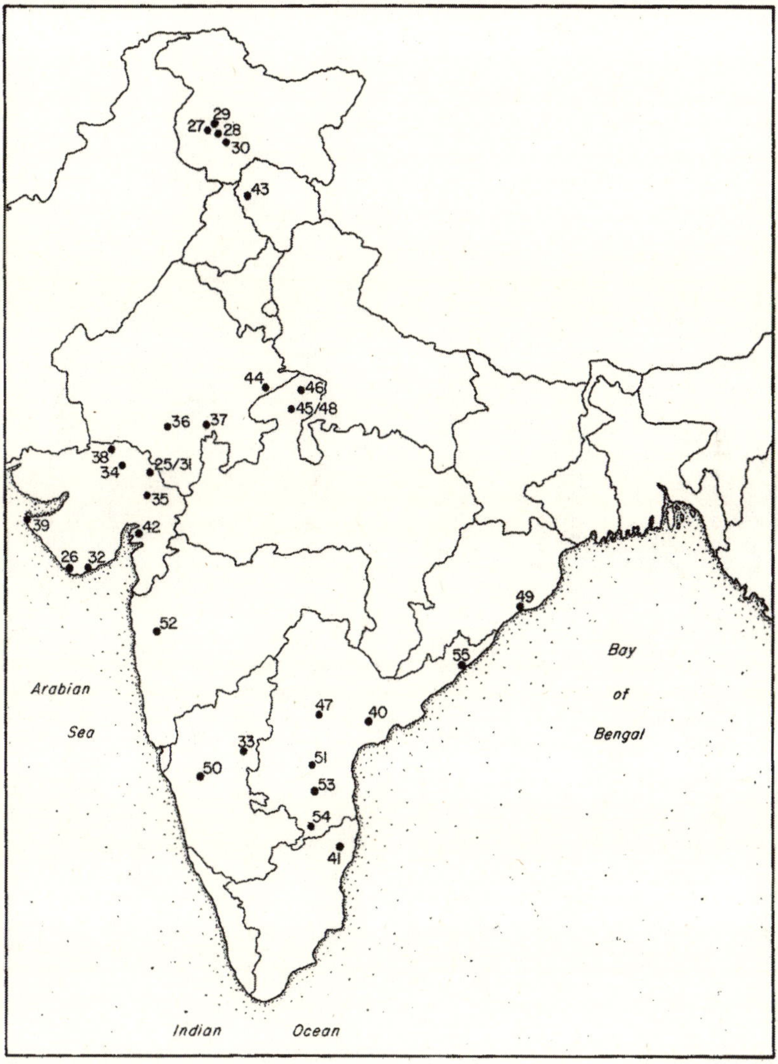

Map 2. Temple Desecrations, 1394–1600: The Growth of Regional Sultanates

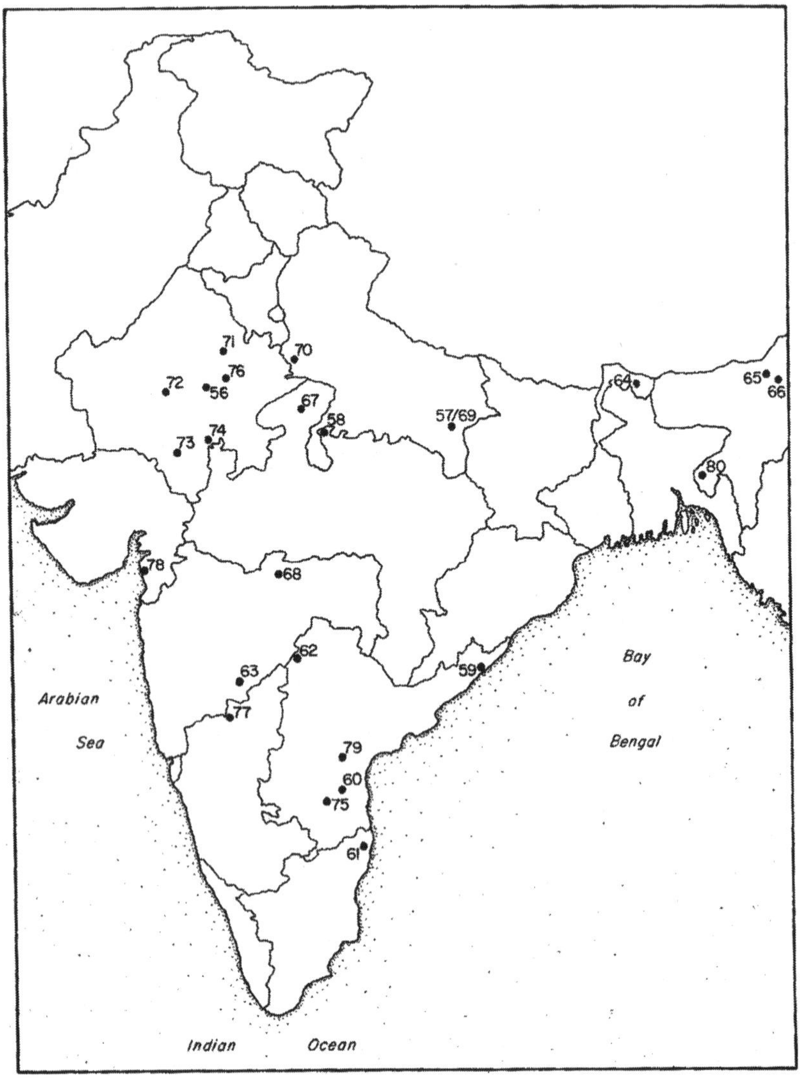

Map 3. Temple Desecrations, 1600–1760: Expansion and Reassertions of Mughal Authority

Table 1. Instances of Temple Desecration, 1192–1760

(e) = emperor; (s) = sultan; (g) = governor; (c) = commander; (p) = crown prince. For numbers 1–24, see Map 1. For numbers 25–55, see map 2. For numbers 56–80 see map 3.

No.	*Date*	*Site*	*District*	*State*	*Agent*	*Source*
1	1193	Ajmer	Ajmer	Rajasthan	Md. Ghuri (s)	23: 215
2	1193	Samana	Patiala	Punjab	Aibek (g)	23: 216-17
3	1193	Kuhram	Karnal	Haryana	Aibek (g)	23: 216-17
4	1193	Delhi		Delhi	Md. Ghuri (s)	1(1911): 13; 23: 217,222
5	1194	Kol	Aligarh	Uttar Pradesh	Ghurid army	23: 224
6	1194	Benares	Benares	Uttar Pradesh	Ghurid army	23: 223
7	c. 1202	Nalanda	Patna	Bihar	Bakhtiyar Khalaji (c)	20: 90
8	c. 1202	Odantapuri	Patna	Bihar	Bakhtiyar Khalaji (c)	22: 319; 21: 551-52
9	c. 1202	Vikramasila	Saharsa	Bihar	Bakhtiyar Khalaji (c)	22: 319
10	1234	Bhilsa	Vidisha	Madhya Prad.	Iltutmish (s)	21: 621-22
11	1234	Ujjain	Ujjain	Madhya Prad.	Iltutmish (s)	21: 622-23
12	1290	Jhain	Sawai Madhopur	Rajasthan	Jalal al-Din Khalaji (s)	27: 146
13	1292	Bhilsa	Vidisha	Madhya Prad.	‘Ala al-Din Khalaji (g)	27: 148
14	1298-1310	Vijapur	Mehsana	Gujarat	Khalaji invaders	2(1974): 10-12
15	1295	Devagiri	Aurangabad	Maharashtra	‘Ala al-Din Khalaji (g)	24: 543
16	1299	Somnath	Junagadh	Gujarat	Ulugh Khan (c)	25: 75

17	1301	Jhain	Sawai Madhopur	Rajasthan	‘Ala al-Din Khalaji (s)	25: 75-76
18	1311	Chidambaram	South Arcot	Tamilnadu	Malik Kafur (c)	25: 90-91
19	1311	Madurai	Madurai	Tamilnadu	Malik Kafur (c)	25: 91
20	c. 1323	Warangal	Warangal	Andhra Prad.	Ulugh Khan (p)	33: 1-2
21	c. 1323	Bodhan	Nizamabad	Andhra Prad.	Ulugh Khan (p)	1(1919-20): 16
22	c. 1323	Pillalamarri	Nalgonda	Andhra Prad.	Ulugh Khan (p)	17: 114
23	1359	Puri	Puri	Orissa	Firuz Tughluq (s)	26: 314
24	1392-93	Sainthali	Gurgaon	Haryana	Bahadur K. Nahar (c)	3(1963-64): 146
25	1394	Idar	Sabar-Kantha	Gujarat	Muzaffar Khan (g)	14-3: 177
26	1395	Somnath	Junagadh	Gujarat	Muzaffar Khan (g)	6-4: 3
27	c. 1400	Paraspur	Srinagar	Kashmir	Sikandar (s)	14-3: 648
28	c. 1400	Bijbehara	Srinagar	Kashmir	Sikandar (s)	34: 54
29	c. 1400	Tripuresvara	Srinagar	Kashmir	Sikandar (s)	34: 54
30	c. 1400	Martand	Anantnag	Kashmir	Sikandar (s)	34: 54
31	1400-1	Idar	Sabar-Kantha	Gujarat	Muzaffar Shah (s)	14-3: 181
32	1400-1	Diu	Amreli	Gujarat	Muzaffar Shah (s)	6-4: 5
33	1406	Manvi	Raichur	Karnataka	Firuz Bahmani (s)	2(1962): 57-58
34	1415	Sidhpur	Mehsana	Gujarat	Ahmad Shah (s)	29: 98-99
35	1433	Delwara	Sabar-Kantha	Gujarat	Ahmad Shah (s)	14-3: 220-21
36	1442	Kumbhalmir	Udaipur	Rajasthan	Mahmud Khalaji (s)	14-3 : 513
37	1457	Mandalgarh	Bhilwara	Rajasthan	Mahmud Khalaji (s)	6-4: 135

38	1462	Malan	Banaskantha	Gujarat	‘Ala al-Din Suhrab (c)	2(1963): 28-29
39	1473	Dwarka	Jamnagar	Gujarat	Mahmud Begdha (s)	14-3: 259-61
40	1478	Kondapalle	Krishna	Andhra Prad.	Md. II Bahmani (s)	6-2: 306
41	c. 1478	Kanchi	Chingleput	Tamilnad	Md. II Bahmani (s)	6-2: 308
42	1505	Amod	Broach	Gujarat	Khalil Shah (g)	1(1933): 36
43	1489-1515	Nagarkot	Kangra	Himachal Prad.	Khawwas Khan (g)	35: 81
44	1507	Utgir	Sawai Madhopur	Rajasthan	Sikandar Lodi (s)	14-1: 375
45	1507	Narwar	Shivpuri	Madhya Prad.	Sikandar Lodi (s)	14-1: 378
46	1518	Gwalior	Gwalior	Madhya Prad.	Ibrahim Lodi (s)	14-1: 402
47	1530-31	Devarkonda	Nalgonda	Andhra Prad.	Quli Qutb Shah (s)	6-3: 212
48	1552	Narwar	Shivpuri	Madhya Prad.	Dilawar Khan (g)	4(June 1927): 101-4
49	1556	Puri	Puri	Orissa	Sulaiman Karrani (s)	28: 413-15
50	1575-76	Bankapur	Dharwar	Karnataka	‘Ali ‘Adil Shah (s)	6-3: 82-84
51	1579	Ahobilam	Kurnool	Andhra Prad.	Murahari Rao (c)	6-3: 267
52	1586	Ghoda	Poona	Maharashtra	Mir Md. Zaman (?)	1(1933-34): 24
53	1593	Cuddapah	Cuddapah	Andhra Prad.	Murtaza Khan (c)	6-3: 274
54	1593	Kalihasti	Chitoor	Andhra Prad.	I’tibar Khan (c)	6-3: 277
55	1599	Srikurman	Visakh.	Andhra Prad.	Qutb Shahi general	32-5: 1312
56	1613	Pushkar	Ajmer	Rajasthan	Jahangir (e)	5: 254
57	1632	Benares	Benares	Uttar Pradesh	Shah Jahan (e)	31: 36
58	1635	Orchha	Tikamgarh	Madhya Prad.	Shah Jahan (e)	7: 102-3
59	1641	Srikakulam	Srikakulam	Andhra Prad.	Sher Md. Kh. (c)	3(1953-54): 68-69

60	1642	Udayagiri	Nellore	Andhra Prad.	Ghazi ‘All (c)	8: 1385-86
61	1653	Poonamalle	Chingleput	Tamilnadu	Rustam b. Zulfiqar (c)	l(1937-38): 53n2
62	1655	Bodhan	Nizamabad	Andhra Prad.	Aurangzeb (p, g)	1(1919-20: 16
63	1659	Tuljapur	Osmanabad	Maharashtra	Afzal Khan (g)	16: 9-10
64	1661	Kuch Bihar	Kuch Bihar	West Bengal	Mir Jumla (g)	9: 142-43
65	1662	Devalgaon	Sibsagar	Assam	Mir Jumla (g)	9: 154,156-57
66	1662	Garhgaon	Sibsagar	Assam	Mir Jumla (g)	36: 249
67	1664	Gwalior	Gwalior	Madhya Prad.	Mu’tamad Khan (g)	10: 335
68	1667	Akot	Akola	Maharashtra	Md. Ashraf (c)	2(1963): 53-54
69	1669	Benares	Benares	Uttar Pradesh	Aurangzeb (e)	11: 65-68; 13: 88
70	1670	Mathura	Mathura	Uttar Pradesh	Aurangzeb (e)	12: 57-61
71	1679	Khandela	Sikar	Rajasthan	Darab Khan (g)	12: 107; 18: 449
72	1679	Jodhpur	Jodhpur	Rajasthan	Khan Jahan (c)	18: 786; 12: 108
73	1680	Udaipur	Udaipur	Rajasthan	Rahullah Khan (c)	15: 129-30; 12: 114-15
74	1680	Chitor	Chitorgarh	Rajasthan	Aurangzeb (e)	12: 117
75	1692	Cuddapah	Cuddapah	Andhra Prad.	Aurangzeb (e)	1(1937-38): 55
76	1697-98	Sambhar	Jaipur	Rajasthan	Shah Sabz ‘Ali (?)	19: 157
77	1698	Bijapur	Bijapur	Karnataka	Hamid al-Din Khan (c)	12: 241
78	1718	Surat	Surat	Gujarat	Haidar Quli Khan (g)	1(1933): 42
79	1729	Cumbum	Kurnool	Andhra Prad.	Muhammad Salih (g)	2(1959-60): 65
80	1729	Udaipur	West	Tripura	Murshid Quli Khan (g)	30: 7

Sources:

1. *Epigraphia Indo-Moslemica.*
2. *Epigraphia Indica, Arabic and Persian Supplement.*
3. *Annual Report of Indian Epigraphy.*
4. *Indian Antiquary.*
5. Jahangir, *Tuzuk-i-Jahangiri,* vol. 1, trans. A. Rogers (Delhi, 1968).
6. Firishta, *Tarikh-i Firishta,* trans. J. Briggs, *History of the Rise of the Mahomedan Power in India* (Calcutta, 1971), 4 vols.
7. Kanbo, *'Amal-i Salih* (Lahore, 1967), vol. 2.
8. A. Butterworth and V. Chetty, *A Collection of the Inscriptions on Copper-Plates and Stones in the Nellore District* (Madras, 1905), vol. 3.
9. Khafi Khan, *Khafi Khan's History of 'Alamgir,* trans. S. Moinul Haq (Karachi, 1975).
10. A. Cunningham, *Four Reports Made during 1862-65* (Varanasi, 1972).
11. S. N. Sinha, *Subah of Allahabad under the Great Mughals* (New Delhi, 1974).
12. Saqi Must'ad Khan, *Ma'asir-i 'Alamgiri,* trans. J. Sarkar (Calcutta, 1947).
13. Saqi Must'ad Khan, *Ma'asir-i 'Alamgiri* (Calcutta, 1871).
14. Nizamuddin Ahmad, *Tabaqat-i Akbari,* trans. B. De (Calcutta, 1973), 3 vols.
15. Ishwardas Nagar, *Futuhat-i 'Alamgiri,* trans. T. Ahmad (Delhi, 1978).
16. Surendranath Sen (ed. and trans.), *Siva Chhatrapati* (Calcutta, 1920), vol. 1.
17. P. Sreenivasachar, ed., *Corpus of Inscriptions in the Telingana Districts ofH.E.M. the Nizam's Dominions,* pt. 2 (Hyderabad, 1940).
18. Shah Nawaz Khan, *Ma'athir-ul-Umara,* vol. 1, trans. H. Beveridge (Patna, 1979).
19. Z. A. Desai, *Published Muslim Inscriptions of Rajasthan* (Jaipur, 1971).
20. G. Roerich, trans. *Biography of Dharmaswamin* (Patna, 1959).
21. Minhaj-i Siraj, *Tabakat-i Nasiri,* vol. 1, trans. H. Raverty (New Delhi, 1970).
22. Debiprasad Chattopadhyaya, ed., *Taranatha's History of Buddhism in India* (Calcutta, 1980).
23. Hasan Nizami, *Taj al-Ma'asir,* in Henry M. Elliot and John Dowson, eds., *The History of India as Told by Its Own Historians* (Allahabad: Kitab Mahal, n.d.), vol. 2.
24. Amir Khusrau, *Miftah al-Futuh* in Elliot and Dowson, *History of India,* vol. 3.
25. Amir Khusrau, *Khaza'in al-Futuh,* in Elliot and Dowson, *History,* vol. 3.
26. Shams-i Siraj, *Tarikh-i Firuz Shahi,* in Elliot and Dowson, *History,* vol. 3.
27. Zia al-Din Barani, *Tarikh-i Firuz Shahi,* Elliot and Dowson, *History,* vol. 3.
28. Khwajah Ni'mat Allah, *Tarikh-i Khan-Jahani wa makhzan-i-Afghani* (Dacca, 1960), vol. 1.
29. Sikandar bin Muhammad, *Mirat-i Sikandari,* in E. C. Bayley, *Local Muhammadan Dynasties: Gujarat,* ed. N. Singh (New Delhi, 1970).
30. Azad al-Husaini, *Nau-Bahar-i Murshid Quli Khani,* trans., Jadu Nath Sarkar, *Bengal Nawabs* (1952; reprint, Calcutta, 1985).
31. 'Abd al-Hamid Lahori, *Badshah-nama,* in Elliot and Dowson, *History,* vol. 7.
32. *South Indian Inscriptions* (New Delhi: Archeological Survey of India).
33. George Michell, "City as Cosmograph," *South Asian Studies* 8 (1992).
34. Jonaraja, *Rajatarangini,* ed. S. L. Sadhu, trans. J. C. Dutt (New Delhi, 1993).
35. Iqtidar Husain Siddiqui, trans., *Waqi'at-e-Mushtaqui of Shaikh Rizq Ullah Mushtaqui* (New Delhi, 1993).
36. Jagadish Narayan Sarkar, *Life of Mir Jumla* (Calcutta, 1952).

Notes

1. See Sita Ram Goel, *Hindu Temples: What Happened to Them?* vol. 1, *A Preliminary Survey* (New Delhi: Voice of India, 1990); vol. 2, *The Islamic Evidence* (New Delhi: Voice of India, 1991).

2. Henry M. Elliot and John Dowson, trans., and eds., *The History of India as Told by Its Own Historians*, 8 vols. (1849; Allahabad: Kitab Mahal, n.d.), l: xxi.

3. Ibid., l:xvi.

4. Ibid., l:xxii, xxvii.

5. K. A. Nizami, ed., *Politics and Society during the Early Medieval Period: Collected Works of Professor Mohammad Habib*, 2 vols. (New Delhi: People's Publishing House, 1974), 1:12.

6. Goel, *Hindu Temples*, 2:115-16. Goel does, however, consider it more likely that the event took place during the reign of Raja Bhoja II in the late thirteenth century than during that of Raja Bhoja I in the eleventh century.

7. G. Yazdani, "The Inscription of the Tomb of 'Abdullah Shah Changal at Dhar," *Epigraphia Indo-Moslemica* (1909): 1-5.

8. A good summary of the political history of this period is found in Andre Wink, *Al-Hind: The Making of the Indo-Islamic World*, vol. 2: *The Slave Kings and the Islamic Conquest, 11th-13th Centuries* (Leiden: Brill, 1997), 111-49.

9. 'Utbi, *Tarikh-i Yamini*, in Elliot and Dowson, *History of India*, 2:22. For a Persian translation of 'Utbi's original Arabic, made in 1206, see Abu Sharaf Nasih al-Jurfadqani, *Tarjuma-yi Tarikh-i Yamini* (Tehran: Bangah-i Tarjomeh va Nashr-i Kitab, 1926-27), 31.

10. C. E. Bosworth, *The Later Ghaznavids, Splendour and Decay: The Dynasty in Afghanistan and Northern India, 1040-1186* (1977; reprint, New Delhi: Munshiram Manoharlal, 1992), 32, 68.

11. Mahmud did not hesitate to sack Muslim cities. His plunder of the Iranian city of Ray in 1029 brought him 500,000 dinars' worth of jewels, 260,000 dinars in coined money, and over 30,000 dinars' worth of gold and silver vessels. India, however, possessed far more wealth than the more sparsely populated Iranian plateau. Somnath alone brought in twenty million dinars' worth of spoil. C. E. Bosworth, *The Ghaznavids: Their Empire in Afghanistan and Eastern Iran, 994-1040* (Edinburgh: Edinburgh University Press, 1963), 78.

12. 'Ali Akbar Fayyaz, ed., *Tarikh-i Baihaqi* (Mashshad: University of Mashshad, 1971), 517. The contemporary historian Baihaqi recorded the first attack on Benares conducted by a Muslim army, carried out in 1033 by the Ghaznavid governor of Lahore. "He marched out with his warriors and the army of Lahore," wrote Baihaqi, "and exacted ample tribute from the Thakurs. He

crossed the river Ganges and went down the left bank. Unexpectedly (*nā-gāh*) he arrived at a city which is called Banaras, and which belonged to the territory of Gang. Never had a Muslim army reached this place. . . . The markets of the drapers, perfumers, and jewelers were plundered, but it was impossible to do more. The people of the army became rich, for they all carried off gold, silver, perfumes, and jewels, and got back in safety." Baihaqi, *Tarikh-i Baihaqi*, in Elliot and Dowson, *History of India*, 2:123-24.

13. "*Jahān-rā ki asās-i matīn basta-and, bi iqdām-i mardān-i dīn basta-and. Bi har kishwarī hast ṣāḥib-dilī, bi har 'arṣat hast bā ḥāṣilī. Bi har mulk garchi amīrī būd, walī dar panāh-i faqīrī būd.*" 'Abd al-Malik 'Isami, *Futuh us-Salatin by 'Isami*, ed. A. S. Usha (Madras: University of Madras, 1948), 455; Agha Mahdi Husain, ed. and trans., *Futuh us-Salatin, or Shah Namah-i Hind of 'Isami*, 3 vols. (Bombay: Asia Publishing House, 1967), 3:687.

14. Ibid., text, 466; trans. 3:702.

15. Ibid., text, 456, 458; trans., 3:689, 690-92. "As soon as that holy man of virtue [Nizam al-Din Auliya] departed from Delhi to the other world," he wrote, "the country, in general, and the city, in particular, fell into a turmoil and were subjected to ruin and destruction."

16. See Simon Digby, "The Sufi Shaikh as a Source of Authority in Mediaeval India," in Marc Gaborieau, ed., *Islam and Society in South Asia*, in *Purusartha* 9 (Paris: Ecole des Hautes Etudes en Sciences Sociales, 1986), 69-70.

17. 'Isami, *Futuh us-Salatin*, text, 7-8; trans., 1:11-13.

18. Richard M. Eaton, *The Rise of Islam and the Bengal Frontier, 1204-1760* (Berkeley: University of California Press, 1993), 86, 91.

19. Muhammad Qasim Firishta, *Tarikh-i Firishta*, trans. John Briggs, in *History of the Rise of the Mahomedan Power in India*, 4 vols. (1829; reprint, Calcutta: Editions Indian, 1966), 4:4.

20. Zafar Hasan, "The Inscriptions of Dhar and Mandu," *Epigraphia Indo-Moslemica* (1909), 12 (*murīd-i shai<u>kh</u>-i ṭarīqat-i Naṣīr-i Dīn Maḥmūd, ki būd maljā-i autād wa marjā'-i abdāl*).

21. Iqtidar Husain Siddiqui, "The Early Chishti Dargahs," in Christian W. Troll, ed., *Muslim Shrines in India: Their Character, History, and Significance* (Delhi: Oxford University Press, 1989), 21.

22. Catherine B. Asher, *Architecture of Mughal India*, vol. 1:4 of *The New Cambridge History of India* (Cambridge: Cambridge University Press, 1992), 34-35, 51, 100, 134, 174, 215, 260, 293, 307, 310.

23. P. M. Currie, *The Shrine and Cult of Mu'in al-Din Chishti of Ajmer* (Delhi: Oxford University Press, 1992), 100.

24. 'Abd al-Qadir Badauni, *Muntakhab al-tawarikh*, vol. 2, trans. W. H. Lowe (1899; reprint, Delhi: Idarah-i Adabiyat-i Delli, 1973), 243.

25. It has been noted recently that the *qawwālī* protocols observed during the annual *'urs* ceremonies at Ajmer, which commemorate the death of Mu'in al-Din Chishti, "betray the impact of Mughal court etiquette. The diwan, dressed in Mughal fashion, represents in fact the Mughal king rather than a religious dignitary, and comes escorted by the torch-bearers and mace-bearers wearing Mughal costumes. He takes his seat on the cushion (*gadela*) under a special tent (*dalbadal*) erected for the occasion....On his arrival in the shrine the diwan kisses the tomb and offers flowers, and then one of the khadims, who happens to be his *wakil*, like the other pilgrims, ties a *dastār* (turban) over his head, spreads the cloth sheet over his bowed head, prays for him, and then gives him tabarruk, consisting of flowers, sandal and sweets....Then he [the diwan] sits down and the *fatiha khwans*, who are permanently and hereditarily employed, recite the fatiha, as well as prayers for the sovereign (*badshah-i Islam*), the diwan, the mutawalli and other officials, and for the general public." Syed Liyaqat Hussain Moini, "Rituals and Customary Practices at the Dargah of Ajmer" in Christian Troll, ed., *Muslim Shrines in India: Their Character, History, and Significance* (Delhi: Oxford University Press, 1989), 72,74.

26. Wink, *Al-Hind*, 2:324.

27. "The need to link one's royal origins to religious and divine forces led to the extraordinary temple building of this period." B. D. Chattopadhyaya, "Historiography, History, and Religious Centers: Early Medieval North India, circa A.D. 700-1200," in Vishakha N. Desai and Darielle Mason, eds., *Gods, Guardians, and Lovers: Temple Sculptures from North India, A.D. 700-1200* (New York: Asia Society Galleries, 1993), 40.

28. Michael Willis suggests that one of the reasons the imperial Pratiharas did not build great monumental temple complexes was precisely their determination to avoid the localization of sovereign power that temples necessarily projected. According to this reasoning, the most active patrons of temple construction in this period were subordinate kings who did not have such vast imperial pretensions as did the Pratiharas. Willis, "Religion and Royal Patronage in North India," in Desai and Mason, eds., *Gods, Guardians, and Lovers*, 58-59.

29. Richard H. Davis, *Lives of Indian Images* (Princeton: Princeton University Press, 1997), 122, 137-38. Davis here cites David D. Shulman: "A divine power is felt to be present naturally on the spot. The texts are therefore concerned with the manner in which this presence is revealed and with the definition of its specific attributes." Shulman, *Tamil Temple Myths: Sacrifice and Divine Marriage in the South Indian Saiva Tradition* (Princeton: Princeton University Press, 1980), 48. Emphasis mine.

30. Cited in Davis, *Lives*, 53.

31. Davis, *Lives*, 51-83, passim. The same pattern continued after the Turkish conquest of India. In the 1460s, Kapilendra, the founder of the Suryavamshi Gajapati dynasty in Orissa, sacked both Saiva and Vaishnava temples in the Kaveri delta in the course of wars of conquest in the Tamil country. See Phillip B. Wagoner, *Tidings of the King: A Translation and Ethnohistorical Analysis of the Rāya-vācakamu* (Honolulu: University of Hawaii Press, 1993), 146. Somewhat later, in 1514, Krishna Deva Raya looted an image of Bala Krishna from Udayagiri, which he had defeated and annexed to his growing Vijayanagara state. Six years later he acquired control over Pandharpur, where he seems to have looted the Vittala image and carried it back to Vijayanagara, with the apparent purpose of ritually incorporating this area into his kingdom. Davis, *Lives*, 65, 67.

32. In the late eleventh century, the Kashmiri king, Harsha, even raised the plundering of temples to an institutionalized activity, and in the late twelfth and early thirteenth centuries, while Turkish rulers were establishing their rule in North India, kings of the Paramara dynasty were attacking and plundering Jain temples in Gujarat. See Romila Thapar, Harbans Mukhia, and Bipan Chandra, *Communalism and the Writing of Indian History* (Delhi: People's Publishing House, 1969), 14, 31.

33. Willis, "Religion and Royal Patronage," 59.

34. In 1788, for example, the author of the *Riyaz al-Salatin* claimed that Muhammad Bakhtiyar demolished local temples after he conquered Bengal in 1204, although no contemporary evidence suggests that he did so. Ghulam Hussain Salim, *Riyaz us-Salatin: A History of Bengal*, trans. Abdus Salam (1903; reprint, Delhi: Idarah-i Adabiyat-i Delli, 1975), 64. Even contemporary sources could make false claims. An inscription on a mosque in Bidar, dated 1670, claims that the Mughal governor, Mukhtar Khan, had destroyed a temple and built the mosque on its site. "But as a matter of fact," noted the epigraphist who published the inscription, "the mosque is a new construction, and the Hindu shrine [to the lion-god Narasimha] which existed inside the rock does not seem to have been disturbed, for it still survives." *Epigraphia Indo-Moslemica*, 1927-28 (Calcutta: Government of India, 1931), 32.

35. Entry for the date 1688 in "Hindu Timeline," *Hinduism Today* (December 1994), cited in Cynthia Talbot, "Inscribing the Other, Inscribing the Self: Hindu-Muslim Identities in Pre-Colonial India," *Comparative Studies in Society and History* 37, no. 4 (October 1995): 692.

36. In 1247, Balban, the future sultan of Delhi, had recommended raiding Indian states for precisely this purpose. See Minhaj-i Siraj Juzjani, *Tabakat-i Nasiri*, 2 vols., trans. H. G. Raverty (1881; New Delhi: Oriental Books Reprint Corp., 1970), 2:816.

37. The notion that Babur's officer Mir Baqi destroyed a temple dedicated to Rama's birthplace at Ayodhya and then got the emperor's sanction to build a mosque on the site—the notorious Baburi Masjid—was elaborated in 1936

by S. K. Banerji. However, the author offered no evidence that there had ever been a temple at this site, much less that it had been destroyed by Mir Baqi. The mosque's inscription records only that Babur had ordered the construction of the mosque, which was built by Mir Baqi and was described as "the place of descent of celestial beings" (*mahbiṭ-i qudsiyān*). This commonplace rhetorical flourish in Persian can hardly be construed as referring to Rama, especially since it is the mosque itself that is so described, and not the site or any earlier structure on the site. See S. K. Banerji, "Babur and the Hindus," *Journal of the United Provinces Historical Society* 9 (1936): 76-83.

38. For example, a 1406 inscription records that after Sultan Firuz Shah Bahmani had defeated the forces of Vijayanagara in the much-contested Raichur doab region, "a mosque has been converted out of a temple as a sign of religion." It then records that the sultan himself had "conquered this fort by the firm determination of his mind in a single attack (lit. on horseback). After the victory, the chief of chiefs, Safdar (lit. the valiant commander) of the age, received (the charge of) the fort." *Epigraphia Indica, Arabic and Persian Supplement*, 1962 (Delhi: Manager of Publications, 1964), 57-58.

39. Briggs, *Rise of Mahomedan Power*, 3:267. The temple's political significance, and hence the necessity of desecrating it, would have been well understood by Murahari Rao, himself a Marathi Brahman.

40. Khwajah Ni'mat Allah, *Tarikh-i Khan Jahani wa Makhzan-i-Afghani*, ed. S. M. Imam al-Din (Dacca: Asiatic Society of Pakistan, 1960), 1:413-15; Abu'l-Fazl, *Akbar-nama*, trans. Henry Beveridge (reprint, New Delhi: Ess Ess, 1979), 2:381-82, 480.

41. S. Moinul Haq, trans., *Khafi Khan's History of 'Alamgir* (Karachi: Pakistan Historical Society, 1975), 142-43.

42. P. B. Desai, "Kalyana Inscription of Sultan Muhammad, Saka 1248," *Epigraphia Indica* 32 (1957-58): 165-68.

43. Ibn Battuta, *Travels in Asia and Africa, 1324-1354*, trans. H. A. R. Gibb (1929; New Delhi: Oriental Books Reprint Corp., 1986), 214.

44. S. L. Sadhu, ed., *Medieval Kashmir, Being a Reprint of the Rajataranginis of Jonaraja, Shrivara, and Shuka*, trans. J. C. Dutt (1898; reprint, New Delhi: Atlantic Publishers and Distributors, 1993), 44-45.

45. Nizamuddin Ahmad, *Tabaqat-i-Akbari*, trans. B. De, 3 vols. (Calcutta: Bibliotheca Indica, 1927–39), 1:386.

46. A useful discussion of Mahmud, his legend, and the question of iconoclasm prior to the establishment of Islamic states is found in Davis, *Lives*, chaps. 3 and 6.

47. Abu'l-Fazl 'Allami, *A'in-i Akbari*, 2nd ed., vol. 3, trans. H. S. Jarrett, ed. Sir Jadunath Sarkar (Calcutta: Asiatic Society of Bengal, 1927; New Delhi: Oriental Books Reprint Corp., 1977-78), 377.

48. Catherine B. Asher, "The Architecture of Raja Man Singh: A Study of Sub-Imperial Patronage," in Barbara Stoler Miller, ed., *The Powers of Art: Patronage in Indian Culture* (Delhi: Oxford University Press, 1992), 183-201.

49. P. Acharya, "Bruton's Account of Cuttack and Puri," *Orissa Historical Research Journal* 10, no. 3 (1961): 46.

50. *Journal of the Asiatic Society of Bengal* (1911): 689-90. Order to Abu'l-Hasan in Benares, dated Feb. 28,1659. My translation. The "continuance of the empire," of course, was always forefront on the minds of the Mughals, regardless of what religious functionary was praying to which deity.

51. "*Az rū-yi shar'-i sharīf wa millat-i munīf muqarrar chunīn ast, ki dairhāyi dīrīn bar andākht nashavad, wa but-kada-hā tāza banā nayābad.*" Ibid., my translation.

52. See Eaton, *Rise of Islam*, 184-85, 263.

53. Surendra Nath Sinha, *Subah of Allahabad under the Great Mughals* (New Delhi: Jamia Millia Islamia, 1974), 65-68; Asher, *Architecture*, 254, 278; Saqi Must'ad Khan, *Ma'athir-i 'Alamgiri* (Calcutta: Bibliotheca Indica, 1871), 88.

54. Saqi Must'Ad Khan, *Ma'asir-i 'Alamgiri*, trans. Jadunath Sarkar (Calcutta, 1947), 57-61; Asher, *Architecture*, 254.

55. See Goel, *Hindu Temples*, 2:78-79, 83; Sri Ram Sharma, *The Religious Policy of the Mughal Emperors*, 2nd ed. (London: Asia Publishing House, 1962), 132-33; Athar Ali, *The Mughal Nobility under Aurangzeb* (Bombay: Asia Publishing House, 1966), 98n.

56. Saqi Must'Ad Khan, *Ma'athir-i 'Alamgiri*, text, 81. My translation. "*Aḥkām-i Islām-nizām ba nāzimān-i kull-i ṣubajāt ṣādir shud ki mudāris wa mu'ābid-i bīdīnīn dast-khwash-i inhidām sāzand, wa ba ta'kīd-i akīd ṭaur-i dars-o-tadrīs wa rasm-i shayū'-i madhāhib-i kufr-āyīnān bar andāzand.*" Cf. Saqi Must'ad Khan, *Ma'asir-i 'Alamgiri: A History of the Emperor Aurangzeb-Alamgiri*, trans. Sir Jadunath Sarkar (Lahore: Suhail Academy, 1981), 51-52.

57. Saqi Must'ad Khan, *Ma'athir-i 'Alamgiri*, 81. "*Ba 'Arz-i khudāvand-i dīn-parvar rasīd ki dar ṣūba-yi Thatta wa Multān khuṣūṣ Banāras brahminān-i baṭṭālat-nishān dar mudāris-i muqarrar ba tadrīs-i kutub-i bāṭila ishtighāl dārand, wa rāghibān wa ṭālibān az hunūd wa musulmān musāfat-hāyi ba 'īda üaiy numūda, jihat-i taḥṣīl-i 'ulūm-i shūm nazd-i ān jamā'At-i gumrāh mīāyand.*" Cf. Sir Jadunath Sarkar, trans., *Ma'asir-i 'Alamgiri*, 51.

58. Consider the swift and brutal punishment of Baha al-Din Gurshasp, a high-ranking officer in Tughluq imperial service and a governor in the Deccan. In 1327, Gurshasp joined forces with the raja of Kampila in an unsuccessful rebellion against Sultan Muhammad bin Tughluq. When captured, the raja, who had never sworn allegiance to Tughluq authority, got the relatively light punishment of a beheading. But the rebel governor, who was not only a former Tughluq officer but the emperor's first cousin, was spat upon by his female relatives and flayed alive; then his skin was stuffed with straw and paraded throughout the imperial provinces as a cautionary tale to the public, while his body was mixed with rice and fed to elephants. See 'Isami, *Futuhu's-Salatin*, trans., 3:658-89; Mahdi Husain, trans., *The Rehla of lbn Battuta* (India, Maldive Islands, and Ceylon) (Baroda: Oriental Institute, 1953), 96. As a final indignity to Gurshasp, we are told by Ibn Battuta that the elephants refused to eat the meal that had been mixed with the rebel's body.

59. Eaton, *Rise of Islam*, 176-77.

60. Muzaffar Alam, "Assimilation from a Distance: Confrontation and Sufi Accommodation in Awadh Society," in R. Champakalakshmi and S. Gopal, eds., *Tradition, Dissent, and Ideology: Essays in Honour of Romila Thapar* (Delhi: Oxford University Press, 1996), 177n.

61. Examples of mosque desecrations are strikingly few in number. In 1697-98 in Sambhar, in Rajasthan's Jaipur District, Shah Sabz 'Ali built a mosque on the site of a temple. In the reign of Shah 'Alam (1707-12), however, non-Muslims came to dominate the region and demolished the mosque, which was subsequently rebuilt in the reign of Farrukh Siyar. See Z. A. Desai, *Published Muslim Inscriptions of Rajasthan* (Jaipur, 1971), 157. Similarly, there is evidence that in 1680, during Aurangzeb's invasion of Rajasthan, the Rajput chief Bhim Singh, seeking to avenge the emperor's recent destruction of temples in Udaipur and elsewhere, raided Gujarat and plundered Vadnagar, Vishalnagar, and Ahmedabad, in the latter place destroying thirty smaller mosques and one large one. See *Raja-sumudra-prasasti*, ch. 22, verse 29, an inscription composed ca. 1683, which appears in Shyamaldas Kaviraj, *Vir Vinod* (Udaipur: Rajayantralaya, 1886); cited in R. C. Majumdar, ed., *The Mughal Empire* (Bombay: Bharatiya Vidya Bhavan, 1974), 351.

62. One can hardly imagine the central focus of a mosque's ritual activity, the prayer niche (*mihrab*), being taken out of the structure and paraded around a Muslim capital by way of displaying Allah's co-sovereignty over an Indo-Muslim ruler's kingdom, in the manner that the ritual focus of a royal temple, the image of the state deity, was paraded around many premodern Hindu capitals in elaborate car festivals.

63. Aiming to cast earlier invaders or rulers in the role of zealous and puritanical heroes, later chroniclers occasionally attributed to such figures the desecration of staggering numbers of temples. Mahmud of Ghazni, for example, is said to have destroyed 10,000 temples in Kanauj and 1,000 in Mathura, his grandson

Ibrahim 1,000 in the Delhi Doab and another 1,000 in Malwa, Aibek 1,000 in Delhi, and Muhammad Ghuri another 1,000 in Benares—figures that Hindu nationalists like Sita Ram Goel have accepted at face value. Goel, *Hindu Temples*, 269.

64. 'Isami, *Futuhu's Salatin*, trans., 1: 66-67.

65. Davis, *Lives*, 71-76.

66. Husain, *Rehla of lbn Battuta*, 4.

67. Sebastiao Manrique, *Travels of Fray Sebastien Manrique, 1629-1643*, trans. E. Luard and H. Hosten, 2 vols. (Oxford: Hakluyt Society, 1927), 1:77.

68. Acharya, "Burton's Account of Cuttack and Puri," 46.

69. See Phillip B. Wagoner, "'Sultan among Hindu Kings': Dress, Titles, and the Islamicization of Hindu Culture at Vijayanagara," *Journal of Asian Studies* 55, no. 4 (November 1996): 851-80; Wagoner, "Harihara, Bukka, and the Sultan: The Delhi Sultanate in the Political Imagination of Vijayanagara," in David Gilmartin and Bruce B. Lawrence (eds.), *Beyond Turk and Hindu: Rethinking Religious Identities in Islamicate South Asia* (New Delhi: India Research Press, 2002).

70. See Wink, *Al-Hind*, 2: 294-333.

71. See Talbot, "Inscribing the Other," 701.

72. Brajadulal Chattopadhyaya, *Representing the Other? Sanskrit Sources and the Muslims* (New Delhi: Manohar, 1998), 49-50, 53, 60, 84.

Islam, Iconoclasm and the Early Indian Mosque

Finbarr B. Flood

1. Introduction[1]

Most accounts of the destruction of the Bamiyan Buddhas by the former Taliban regime of Afghanistan invoked the widespread idea that Muslims are implacably hostile to figural imagery, situating the demise of the Buddhas within a long culturally determined tradition of image destruction. Despite abundant evidence for the espousal of figural art in many parts of the Islamic world from the time of the Prophet onwards, in both scholarly and popular discourse, 'Islamic iconoclasm' generally refers to a quasi-pathological aversion to figuration that is assumed to be an essential and enduring characteristic of Islamic culture, and that is particularly directed towards the religious images of the non-Muslim 'Other'. In this

1 An earlier version of this paper was submitted for publication in Anne McClanan & Jeffrey Johnson (eds.), *Negating the Image: Case Studies of Past Iconoclasms* (Ashgate Press) in the spring of 2002. Both papers are based on a talk presented to the symposium Exploring the Frontiers of Islamic Art at MIT, Cambridge, Mass., in May 2001. An extended discussion of the issues raised here will appear in my forthcoming book on the Ghurids and South Asia. The observations offered here are based on a very brief visit to the mosques undertaken in 1999, and are therefore of a preliminary nature.

way, acts of iconoclasm undertaken by Muslims (as opposed to Christians, for example) are generally held to be primarily the product of a religious compulsion underwritten by a timeless theology of images, and only secondarily motivated by economic or political factors, if at all.

Such assumptions negate the role of Muslim iconoclasts as historical agents (Ernst 2000:116), obscure the specific socio-political circumstances in which image destruction occurred, and elide regional and historical differences in attitudes to figuration. Those who represented the fate of the Buddhas as the inevitable product of a cultural fixation with images, for example, ignored the fact that they had been celebrated as wonders by Muslim writers for almost a millennium before their destruction. In doing so, they obviated the need to explain what specific changes in the culture and politics of the region (and beyond) had led to the events of March 2001. The ahistoricism that follows from the naturalization of historical acts not only makes for bad scholarship, but reinforces essentialist constructions of Islam that can have a profound political impact in the present.

Among the many problems with traditional constructions of 'Islamic iconoclasm' that one could highlight, this paper focuses on the complex interplay between creation and destruction that characterizes many iconoclastic interventions. It is specifically concerned with the aesthetic implications of iconoclasm in the first mosques constructed after the Muslim conquest of north India in the late twelfth century. Based on empirical observation, it challenges the assumed linkage between the negation of Hindu and Jain images that appeared on architectural elements reused in the construction of the mosques, and the rejection of the artistic traditions which they are assumed to embody. In doing so, it seeks to demonstrate the need for further empirical research on the subject and a re-evaluation of the conceptual framework within which the relationship between Islam, Muslims and images has been articulated.

2. Iconoclasm in the Islamic World

The opposition to figuration in Islam is based not on any Qur'anic injunction, but on various Traditions of the Prophet, the Hadith (Paret 1960; Paret 1968; van Reenen, 1990), whose proscriptions are reinforced by historical accounts of idol-destruction after the conversion of pagan sanctuaries in Arabia for Muslim use (Flood 2002). The two principal objections to figuration in the proscriptive texts are a concern with usurping divine creative powers (Paret 1960: 43-44; Wensinck[-Fahd] 1997: 889), and fear of *shirk*, polytheism and idolatry (Hawting 1999: 22, 49). There is a general consensus in the Traditions forbidding all representations that have shadows (whose defacement is obligatory), and some schools of thought go so far as to liken artists to polytheists (Wensinck-[Fahd] 1997: 889-90). Such proscriptions were undoubtedly a factor in promoting aniconism, or the avoidance of figural imagery (Grabar 1977: 51), but their impact varied widely in time and place. Attitudes towards figuration could change over time, or with the advent of new political regimes with different cultural values.

If attitudes towards figuration in the medieval Islamic world were far from homogenous or monolithic, it is within the context of ritual or sacred space that the proscriptions on figuration had their greatest effect. Although detailed studies of figural ornament in medieval Islamic religious architecture are few and far between (Anatolia being an unusual exception), it is fairly consistently avoided in the decoration of medieval mosques and madrasas. In those mosques where figural ornament did appear (e.g. Pope 1946; Roux 1980), it was generally eschewed in the area around the prayer-niche (*mihrāb*), but even here there are exceptions. Such exceptions include pre-Islamic monuments converted for use as mosques, in which figural ornament was sometimes left intact (Pedersen 1991: 650).

In addition to the promotion of aniconism (at least at a normative or ideal level), the proscriptions on figuration led to a lingering unease that could motivate acts of iconoclasm (the destruction or mutilation of existing figural imagery) by pious individuals or, more rarely, the medieval state. Such iconoclastic moments might target either the symbols of the 'Other' and/or the art produced during the reigns of Muslim predecessors (Flood 2002, 645). The Hadith offer at least two practical strategies for iconoclasts: perhaps surprisingly, both fall short of total obliteration. Images could either be re-contextualized in a manner that made clear that they were in no way venerated (by reusing figural textiles as floor cushions, for example) or, alternatively, they might be decapitated, so that they became inanimate, that is, devoid of a soul or *rūḥ* (Paret 1960: 46-47; Paret 1976-77: 158, 176; van Reenen 1990: 33, 54). To judge from both textual evidence and surviving objects, these strategies were frequently employed by medieval iconoclasts in the Islamic world (Flood 2002). In many cases defacement (or the mutilation of the affective parts of face such as the eyes and nose) often substituted for decapitation, a practice that finds precedents in early accounts of Prophet Muhammad's iconoclastic activities (Faris 1952: 27). In both manuscript painting and metalwork, a line was sometimes drawn across the throat in a symbolic decapitation (e.g. Petrosyan et al. 1995: 144-55). Occasionally, ritual defilement substituted for physical alteration and was evidently considered sufficient to negate or neutralize the image. It is important to note that such practices are by no means peculiar to the Islamic world: the same focus on the head and face characterizes the work of late antique, medieval and early modern iconoclasts in Europe (Freedberg 1989: 415), where a work of art might "be 'damaged' rather than 'destroyed' in order to make it a token of the violence it was subjected to and of the infamy of anything with which it is associated (Gamboni 1997: 19)." The continued existence of such ritually 'destroyed' images suggests that the dichotomy between creation and destruction that underlies much writing on Islamic iconoclasm offers too reductive a reading of iconoclastic practice. This is the case with the Indian mosques that form the subject of this paper.

3. Iconoclasm and the Early Indian Mosque

There are few areas of the Islamic world where the issue of Islamic iconoclasm has proved as contentious as in South Asia. In traditional South Asian historiography of the colonial and post-colonial periods, the invasions of predominantly Hindu northern India by the armies of Muslim sultans based in Afghanistan during the eleventh and twelfth centuries are characterized as pitting a monolithic indigenous iconophilia against an equally homogeneous Islamic iconophobia, resulting in the destruction of temples and the looting and desecration of religious icons.

Curiously, discussions of Islamic iconoclasm in South Asia have tended to focus on its least tangible aspect, the now vanished portable images whose histories are known primarily through medieval texts (Davis 1997: 88-113). This focus on the intangible reflects a larger historical problem in the study of medieval South Asian cultures, namely the preeminence afforded texts, which frequently provide the lens through which even material remains of the medieval period are viewed (Patel 2000: 325-58; Kumar 2001: 172). Thus, the much more quantifiable evidence for iconoclasm offered by the alteration of images that appeared on architectural elements from Hindu temples reused in certain medieval Indian mosques has escaped detailed examination. Nevertheless, despite the lack of detailed study, the alterations have generally been taken as corroborating textual accounts of a virulent culturally determined iconoclasm,[2] with devastating consequences in the present.

The destruction of the sixteenth-century Babri Mosque at Ayodhya in 1992, which sparked violent inter-communal rioting,

---

2 See, for example, André Wink's analysis of Islamic iconoclasm, in which he cites the destruction of (unnamed) religious monuments in modern Bangladesh and Pakistan as exemplifying the phenomenon seen in twelfth-century India (Wink 1997: 323). There is no discussion of the very different cultural and historical circumstances in which these acts occurred (Partition or the rise of the nation state, for example), and questions of motive and agency are obscured by the assertion of a timeless, theologically motivated cultural compulsion. For a critique of the same phenomenon in relation to Bamiyan see Flood (2002).

was justified by the belief that a temple that once stood on the site had been destroyed by Muslim iconoclasts to make way for the mosque (Guha-Thakurta 1997). Those seeking to provide a rationale for this act of contemporary iconoclasm, and to prepare the ground for future destruction, have drawn directly on colonial and post-colonial scholarship on Indo-Islamic monuments (e.g. Goel 1993). As others have noted, within such scholarship architectural forms, and even their component elements, have traditionally been categorized in ways that assign them fixed sectarian identities as 'Buddhist', 'Hindu' or 'Muslim.' Consequently, the very presence of 'Hindu' material in mosques is assumed to corroborate the generic references to temple destruction that pepper medieval Arabic and Persian textual histories, with little further investigation (Asher 2000: 122; Patel 2000: 311-22; Flood 2001: 155; Kumar 2001: 175).[3] However unwitting, the resulting complicity of scholarship on early Islamic architecture in South Asia in the current wave of anti-Muslim iconoclasm at contested sites is directly proportional to its continuing willingness to embrace the essentialist paradigm of Islamic iconoclasm discussed at the outset.

This paradigm is particularly evident in published discussions of the mosques built in the later twelfth and early thirteenth centuries (roughly between 1175 and 1205), after much of northern India was brought under the control of an eastern Iranian dynasty of Muslim rulers based at Ghur in central Afghanistan. This radical change in the political configuration of South Asia has usually been seen as bringing about a profound rupture in the cultural fabric of the region, the product of a clash between two mutually opposed and incommensurate cultural traditions. Articulated within discussions of the mosques built after the conquest, discussions often strongly colored by issues of colonialism, nationalism, religious fundamentalism, and race (Flood unpublished; Kumar 2001), the

3 There are some notable exceptions to this general tendency. See, for example, Lehmann 1978.

question of responses to the image, and to religious imagery in particular, have served as a touchstone for this division.

At least four mosques built in the wake of the conquest survive. Two of these, the Qutbi mosque at Delhi and the Arhai-din-ka Jhompra Mosque at Ajmer in Rajasthan, bear foundation inscriptions giving respective dates of 587/1192 and 596/1199 (Horovitz 1911-12: 13, 15; Hillenbrand 1988). The inscriptions of the Delhi mosque inform us that it was built by the Turkish commander Qutb al-Din Aybak on the orders of the Ghurid sultan, Muhammad b. Sam [r. 1163-1203] (Horovitz 1911-12: 14; Page 1926: 29). A third mosque, the Shahi-Masjid at Khatu in Rajasthan, is provided with a *mihrāb* (prayer-niche) of virtually identical form to that in the Ajmer mosque, and can be confidently dated to the turn of the twelfth century (Shokoohy & Shokoohy 1993: 107). Finally, the Chaurasi Khamba mosque at Kaman, in the Bayana region of Rajasthan can be ascribed to the patronage of another Turkish commander of the Ghurids, Baha al-Din Tughrul, some time between 1195 and 1210, when he ruled as governor (Shokoohy & Shokoohy 1987).

The basic form of these stone monuments is similar in each case with a monumental projecting entrance (often elevated) leading to a central courtyard with a multi-bayed prayer-hall at its western end and, at Delhi and Kaman, a narrow arcade or *riwāq* surrounding the remaining three sides. The interior spaces are covered by means of corbeled domes and flat slabs supported on trabeate beams borne by pillars composed of discrete sections set vertically on end to achieve the required height. Many (but not all) of these elements have been reused from earlier pre-conquest monuments.

Based on a number of common features, including the use of spolia and their location on what are believed to be the sites of former temples, it has been suggested that such mosques constitute a distinct type, recently dubbed the "conquest mosque," which is associated with the expansion of the frontiers of Islamicate South Asia (Wagoner & Rice 2001: 89-90). The stone mosques built by

Hindu craftsmen for communities of Muslims living in Sind and Gujarat in the eleventh and twelfth centuries, before the Ghurid conquest, make no use of spolia (eg. Shokoohy 1988). Such craftsmen were surely available in major urban centers such as Ajmer and Delhi after the conquest and, as we will see, may even have been involved in the construction of Ghurid mosques from reused materials. The use of spolia even when alternatives were available thus seems to represent a deliberate choice. The fact that the same pattern is repeated later, with mosques of similar form also constructed from spolia built immediately after the conquest of different Indian regions by the Delhi sultans in the 13th and 14th centuries, points to a relationship between the construction of such mosques from spolia and successful campaigns of conquest (Wagoner & Rice 2001: 90-105).

Dale Kinney has noted of spolia in another context that "how the *spolia* were acquired must have been a principal determinant of how they were originally perceived (Kinney 1995: 57)." In the existing discourse on the early Indian mosque, the converse is also true: how the use of spolia is perceived often colors assumptions about the contexts in which they were acquired. In published discussions of the Indo-Ghurid mosques the reused material is either assumed to come from desecrated temples, or the contentious issue of source is side-stepped by attributing the use of spolia rather generically and vaguely to their abundance (Patel 2000: 270). It seems probable that the truth lies somewhere in between. As the range of styles represented in the material indicates, not all the material reused in Indo-Ghurid mosques is of the same date: in fact, some of the material pre-dates the Ghurid conquest by several centuries (Meister 1993: 448). Although not strictly orthodox, the reuse of earlier architectural material was known in north Indian temples (Wink 1997: 322; Dhaky 1998: 127). The reuse of material does not of itself offer evidence for temple desecration, therefore, since some of this material may have been available from ruined structures including (but not restricted to) temples. Other of the spolia reused in the Indo-Ghurid mosques come from more recent structures, however, and their abundance seems to reflect a policy of selective desecration during periods of conquest and military expansion.

Although the phenomenon of iconoclasm in pre-conquest South Asia is usually considered a cultural anomaly, and has therefore never been systematically studied, both image destruction and temple desecration were practiced by 'Hindu' kings before the advent of the Ghurids. Just as divergent attitudes to images existed within Islam, Buddhist, Hindu and Jain images were contested between different sects and faiths in South Asia, sometimes leading to the desecration and destruction of portable icons, or the erasure and mutilation of images in temples and shrines (Golzio 1990; Thapar 1994: 16-18; Wink 1997: 310-11; Flood forthcoming). Other instances of pre-conquest iconoclasm occurred at times of military conquest or political change, and may be seen as reflecting the close inter-relationships between centers of political and religious authority in medieval South Asia. In addition to image destruction, medieval South Asian rulers of the pre-conquest period also desecrated the temples of those that they defeated far more frequently than one might imagine from published discussions of the early Indian mosque (Eaton 2000: 256; Flood forthcoming).

In a recent study of those instances of temple desecration by invading Muslim armies that can be reliably documented, Richard Eaton concludes that "temples had been the natural sites for the contestation of kingly authority well before the coming of the Muslim Turks to India," therefore, "by targeting for desecration those temples that were associated with defeated kings, conquering Turks, when they made their own bid for sovereign domain in India, were subscribing to, even while they were exploiting, indigenous notions of royal legitimacy" (Eaton 2000: 256, 270). As in the pre-Ghurid period, in many cases these were not random acts of destruction, but represented a selective desecration of shrines identified as the power bases of defeated rivals, whose tutelary images were often carried off for display in the victor's capital (Davis 1997: 51-87; Eaton 2000: 256). As an instrument of state policy this practice finds parallels in the practices of pre-conquest Indian rulers. Along with the looting and destruction of religious images, temple desecration therefore appears to have been phenomena of the expanding frontier in pre-Ghurid South Asia. It therefore seems likely that the employment of spolia in the early mosques derives from a complex interweaving of political and economic pragmatism (depriving a rival of the source of his political power, while profiting from the resulting availability of architectural materials). A similar intention can be detected behind the looting of temple elements by pre-conquest Indian kings, who carried the materials off to be incorporated into their own dynastic shrines (Dayalan 1985: 136). This is not to elide important differences in the nuances and political consequences of iconoclastic acts in northern India before and after the Ghurid conquest (Kumar 2001: 159, 161), although even here cultural difference has frequently been over-emphasized (Flood 2002: 650-51; Flood forthcoming), but to emphasize that the principle of image destruction, temple desecration and the reuse of architectural elements in the context of military conquest was by no means as alien to pre-conquest South Asia as is often assumed.

4. Iconoclasm as an Anti-Aesthetic Gesture

Perhaps because of its implied associations with conquest and victory, the reuse of architectural members in Indo-Ghurid mosques has been read as a derogation of 'Indian' tradition, a negative response to the aesthetics of the temple and its emphasis on figuration. In one of the earliest reports on the Quwwat al-Islam or Qutbi Mosque, the Ghurid Friday mosque of Delhi (1192 onwards), the antiquarian Alexander Cunningham noted in 1863 that,

> The general effect of these large rows of made-up columns is certainly rich and pleasing; but this effect is due to the kindly hand of time, which has almost entirely removed the coating of plaster with which the whole

> of these beautifully sculptured pillars were once barbarously covered by the idol-hating Musalmâns (Cunningham 1871: 177).

The question of aesthetic value was thus inversely linked to the iconoclastic impulse in scholarly discourse on this key monument from its inception. This linkage is related to a much broader art historical tendency to privilege originary works over those created from their components (Kinney 1995: 55; Patel 2000: 236). In terms of the Indo-Ghurid mosque, that originary work consists of both the assumed material source, the despoliated temple from which components are drawn, and the conceptual source, the eastern Iranian mosque to which the early Indian mosques are often assumed to be crude (and aesthetically alien) approximations (Welch 1993: 314). In what follows, I want to suggest ways of looking at the Indo-Ghurid mosque that transcend the tendency to privilege some implied original (whether material temple or conceptual mosque), considering the Indo-Ghurid mosque not as a random collection of mutilated fragments, but as a *Gesamtkunstwerk*, and examining the role of iconoclasm in its creation.

Let us turn to the first two of Cunningham's propositions: that the images carved on the reused pillars were covered, hence no aesthetic value was placed on the pillars. The iconoclastic practices envisioned by Cunningham – a spree of image mutilation followed by a swift dose of whitewash – not only have a distinctly Protestant feel to them, but are based on a number of erroneous assumptions. In fact, somewhat ironically, any desire to obscure the decoration of the reused pillars seems to have been subordinated to aesthetic considerations, for the "pleasing effect" that Cunningham noted in the rows of reused pillars was deliberately orchestrated by those responsible for the mosque's construction. At key points in the mosque – around the opening of the eastern entrance onto the courtyard for example - the gray, yellow, and red stones from which the mosque was constructed are arranged so that these colors alternate in horizontal bands. Similar effects were orchestrated by those who arranged the stones reused in the Ghurid Friday Mosque at Ajmer, and the mosque at Kaman in Rajasthan, where one also finds alternating courses of richly carved gray, red and yellow stone. In the careful juxtaposition of different colored stones we see here in embryonic form the polychromatic aesthetic beloved of certain early sultanate monuments, among them the Ala'i-Darwaza at the Qutbi Complex in Delhi. The antecedents of the tradition lie, however, in the pre-conquest temple architecture of north India, where similar arrangements of structural stones to form horizontal bands of polychromy are sometimes found.

The espousal of lithic polychromy is among a number of features common to both temple and mosque, despite the reconfiguration of visual idioms in the latter (Meister 1993: 449). This continuity of tradition suggests that craftsmen trained to build temples were later involved in the construction of Ghurid mosques from their components. Even if these components were plastered in the *post*-Ghurid period, the care taken to achieve such effects only makes sense if the pillars were seen and *not* obscured beneath a coat of plaster when the mosque was built in the twelfth century.[4]

The assertion that the images on the structural members of the Delhi mosque were obscured is thus contradicted by the most cursory examination of the monument, and would appear to be based solely on the belief that images must have been so offensive to the patrons of the mosque that they could not possibly have remained visible. A variant on this idea holds that the figures depicted on reused material were mutilated in "a rather feeble and crude attempt to render the human form unrecognizable" (Grover 1981: 6). Just how feeble, may be seen from the fact that clearly recognizable anthropomorphic figures are to be found throughout

4 There are in fact many examples of Indian mosques in which richly carved reused elements that were originally exposed were later plastered over (e.g. Shokoohy & Shokoohy 2000: 62, figs. 10-11). Even if whitewashed later, the images were not necessarily obscured: both temples and mosques could be whitewashed annually in India without obscuring (or, without any intention to obscure) their decoration.

the mosque (e.g. figure 2). Nevertheless, changes *have* been made to many of the anthropomorphic representations in this and other Ghurid mosques. In the majority of cases these alterations are restricted to the most anthropomorphic features, predominantly facial features such as eyes and noses (figures 1–3), thereby conforming to iconoclastic practice in other areas of the medieval Islamic world (Flood 2002).

Assuming that the majority of the alterations to the images in the Delhi mosque were made at the time that the pillars were reused in the late twelfth century (and broad parallels with the patterns of iconoclasm found in other Indo-Ghurid mosques would seem to support this),[5] we are dealing with something much more than a visceral response to the image. The scale of the undertaking suggests a considerable investment of time and labor: one might even speak of an economics of iconoclasm. Other case studies indicate that the iconoclastic process can be bureaucratic, calculated, and protracted (Bahrani 1995: 367): in the case of the materials reused in Delhi and elsewhere it must have extended over a certain time frame, days at least. We are not dealing therefore with an immediate emotional reaction, but with what appears to have been an orchestrated program of alteration directly related to that which governed the collection and re-assembly of existing architectural materials.

As already noted, it is probable that craftsmen trained in the temple tradition were responsible for the construction of many, if not all, Indo-Ghurid mosques. It is therefore conceivable, if not provable, that these same craftsmen were responsible for altering the figures on reused pillars at the behest of their Ghurid patrons. Many instances of 'Islamic iconoclasm' appear to be the product of a negotiation between iconoclasts and iconophiles, with the latter modifying existing images either for financial remuneration, or to prevent more extensive alterations by those opposed to figuration

5 The mosques at Ajmer and Khatu, which are closely related in terms of their decoration, also represent the most radical expression of both an aniconic and iconoclastic impulse that is much more muted in Delhi and Kaman.

(e.g. Schick 1995: 218-9; Flood, forthcoming). Physical damage to religious icons was considered to preclude their veneration in medieval Hinduism (Davis 1992: 52), a fact noted in medieval Arabic references to Indian iconolatry (Said 1989: 78). In pre-modern societies, iconoclasts frequently considered such physical transformations more effective in neutralizing or negating images if they were undertaken by those who had formerly worshipped or otherwise made use of the altered images. The alteration of the relatively minor deities found on the architectural elements reused in Indo-Ghurid mosques may therefore have functioned as a mode of de-consecration desirable to both Muslim patrons and Hindu craftsmen for different reasons. If the impetus for neutralizing the images came from the patrons of these monuments, the range of ways in which images are altered (from the uncommon total erasure to the ubiquitous gouging of the face: figures 1 & 2) suggests that the specific ways in which it was to be effected were left to the individual craftsman.

Once again, such investment of resources in the relatively minor alterations to the figural imagery only makes sense if those images were originally visible in their altered state and not obscured beneath a layer of stucco. One therefore gets the impression that the alteration of anthropomorphic images derived not from a desire to obscure them, but from a need to neutralize them in a manner that accorded with both textual prescriptions and established iconoclastic practice. This need was contingent upon the decision to reuse pre-carved elements bearing figural ornament in the construction of a mosque. This being so, it is useful to attempt to distinguish here between *instrumental* iconoclasm, in which a particular action is executed in order to achieve a greater goal, and *expressive* iconoclasm, in which the desire to express one's beliefs or give vent to one's feelings is achieved by the act itself (Gregory 1994: 89). In these early Indian mosques, the use of decapitation and defacement by Muslim iconoclasts represents a type of instrumental iconoclasm, for it permitted the survival of pre-existing images in the prescribed way (albeit in altered form) as part of a larger whole. Although the product of changes in attitudes within a religious community rather than shifts in cultural values stemming from political change, an analogous phenomenon may underlie the erasure of images in the Late Antique synagogues of Palestine, which one scholar has ascribed to "the desire to keep using a mosaic or appurtenance after the communal aesthetic changed from one of tolerance for images to one of lessened tolerance or even hostility toward them (Fine 2000: 190)."

Within the post-conquest north Indian mosques, there is little sense that the reuse of temple elements represents a derogation of the Indic traditions that they represent, although this has been generally assumed and frequently asserted. On the contrary, as the careful alternation of colored stones in certain places indicates, established pre-conquest conventions continued to govern the reuse of pre-existing elements, which by and large conforms to the architectural grammar of the Indian temple (Meister 1993: 448). Even elements featuring figural ornament were used right side up in prominent contexts (above exterior window openings, for example [Page 1926: pl. 9c; Dikshit 1944]), while iconoclastic alterations to such figural scenes were relatively restrictive in nature, and did not involve all figures equally, as we shall see shortly. In Ajmer, Delhi, and Khatu reused elements appeared alongside those carved ex novo, with the style of the spolia determining that of the newly carved members (Meister 1972: 57), a phenomenon that "seems to indicate more of a positive response than the traditional scholarly interpretation of a violent extinguishing of a despised tradition (Patel 2000: 322)."

In fact, the positive aesthetic value placed on architectural materials reused in Indo-Ghurid mosques in India needs to be seen in a wider cultural and geographic context. Similar Indic traditions were, for example, espoused in contemporary funerary monuments built for Ghurid patrons in the Indus Valley, which make no use of stone or spolia, but are instead constructed from brick, the established building material in the region. The style of these monuments is closely related to that of the temples of the region, and they appear to represent collaboration between local artisans and those from Ghurid centers in Afghanistan (Flood 2001: 144-8, 157).

Even more remarkable is the evidence for Ghurid architectural tastes and aesthetic values from Afghanistan itself. While Indic elements such as *purnagatha* capitals may be found in the art of the region from the eleventh century (Flood 2002a: 111, pls. 10.5-6), along with decorative and structural techniques that hint at the presence of Indian craftsmen (Fischer 1966: 29; Pinder-Wilson 2001: 157), it is precisely at the height of the Indian conquest at the end of the twelfth century that a vogue for Indic ornament manifests itself most strongly in the Ghurid homeland. The most remarkable testimony to this vogue is the Masjid-i sangi at Larvand in central Afghanistan, a small monument constructed in stone (itself an anomaly in a region where brick was the norm) in an idiom that is closely related to that of contemporary temples in Gujarat and Kathiawar. Whether the Masjid-i sangi was the work of migrant Indian craftsmen or was built with materials taken to Afghanistan from India is not clear (Scarcia & Taddei 1973; Ball 1990), but the proliferation of traditional Indic modes of ornament is also evidenced in a number of other fragmentary late twelfth-century Ghurid monuments (some dated) that make use of standard decorative elements of Indic architecture, among them vase-and-foliage capitals, lotus scrolls, and half-lotus friezes (Flood 2001: 153-54, figs. 42-43). Taken with the evidence of the Indian monuments themselves, the reception of such ornament in the Ghurid heartlands strongly suggests that the material reused in Indo-Ghurid mosques was invested with a positive aesthetic value.

The third and final of Cunningham's assumptions concerns not the specifics of the Indian mosque, but the more general assumption that a virulent iconophobia determined an aggressively negative attitude towards all figural imagery on the part of medieval

Muslims. This idea, first promulgated in colonial era reports on the early Indian mosques, is of course premised on the essentialist discourse discussed at the outset. It continues to have currency, albeit in qualified forms: in a revised edition of the most influential survey book on Islamic art and architecture, the iconoclastic transformations witnessed in the Delhi mosque are ascribed to the "fanatic iconoclasts who formed the backbone of the conquering armies" (Ettinghausen, *et al*. 2001: 163-4). The notion of Ghurid armies as comprised of violent iconoclasts similarly seems to underlie continued assertions that the images on the reused stones were originally covered (Welch 1993: 311), despite the evidence to the contrary within and without the mosque. Seldom is it noted, for example, that, in their Indian coin issues, the Ghurid sultans continued pre-existing types featuring Hindu deities such as Lakshmi and Nandi (Sastri 1937: 495; Flood forthcoming). While it by no means proves that the issue of the image was unproblematic, the minting of such coins certainly reveals a more complex and ambivalent response to figural imagery (even religious imagery) on the part of the Ghurid sultans than one would suspect from reading contemporary chronicles. The glimpse into this liminal space between textual rhetoric and cultural practice provided by the numismatic evidence may be broadened by reference to the specific treatment of the images that appeared contemporaneously on the richly carved stone elements reused in Indo-Ghurid mosques. On closer inspection, many of the mosques that are assumed to embody a visceral loathing of the image in fact offer evidence that undermines the idea of a monolithic Islamic iconoclasm.

By the late twelfth century there was, as previously noted, a long-established aversion to the use of figural imagery in the decoration of a mosque, and the figural representations that appeared on reused material in Indo-Ghurid mosques were indeed considered problematic. Steps were therefore taken to alter some of the existing figural decoration. The alteration of figural sculpture on elements valued for their aesthetic properties is by no means exclusive to

India: the same phenomenon is manifest contemporaneously in the Crusader sculptures reused in the Islamic monuments of Jerusalem after the city had been recaptured in the twelfth century (Jacoby 1992: 21). Moreover, the treatment of images on the material reused in the Indo-Ghurid mosques is closely correlated to the nature of the imaged; the economics of iconoclasm evidently dictated that only those images considered problematic were altered.

The alteration of anthropomorphic imagery is the closest one gets to a monolithic iconoclasm in the Indo-Ghurid mosque, and considerable resources appear to have been expended in neutralizing such imagery. In only a few cases are the alterations so drastic that they amount to the total elimination of the form so that it is no longer recognizable or visible only in shadow outline. In most cases the alteration is restricted to the mutilation of the face or head (figures 1-2). Much less energy was expended on dealing with animal imagery, which is only occasionally altered (as noted by Shokoohy & Shokoohy 1993: 109 and 1996: 335). Certain types of representational imagery, including figural imagery, were thus left untouched in Indo-Ghurid mosques, with elephants, birds, and mythological creatures such as *maqaras* appearing alongside headless torsos and noseless faces. This is particularly evident in the northern porch of the Kaman mosque, richly embellished with reused figural sculpture which has been selectively mutilated, so that elephant heads and the images of mythological creatures are intact, while anthropomorphic images are defaced.

Most remarkable of all, and perhaps by virtue of its perceived apotropaïc properties, the image of the radiant horned lion, the *kīrtimukha* was not only left unaltered, but became as ubiquitous a figure as it had been in pre-Ghurid Buddhist stupas and Hindu temples (Flood, forthcoming). Based on a brief and unscientific headcount, in the Qutbi Mosque, the Ghurid Friday Mosque of Delhi alone the image of the *kīrtimukha* appears more than thirty times on the trabeate lintels that still remain in place (roughly fifty per cent of the original number), and innumerable more times on the reused columns that support them. This survival is not the random product of chance but represents a deliberate choice, for throughout the mosque one can find pillars on which anthropomorphic figures have been defaced while the associated image of the *kīrtimukha* remains intact (figure 3). Even in the mosques at Ajmer and Khatu, where the iconoclastic alterations are most extensive, numerous manifestations of the beast are still intact. In fact, it seems to have been considered such an integral part of the contemporary mosque, that it is found on elements that were apparently carved ex novo for Ghurid mosques in India (at Khatu, for example), and on the entrance and interior beams of the Masjid-i sangi in central Afghanistan, where it features alongside friezes of ducks or geese (*haṃsamithuna*s) similar to those found in contemporary Hindu temples (Scarcia and Taddei 1973: 98, figs. 3-4). The latter serves as a cogent reminder that even figuration was no bar to the assimilation of Indic elements in monuments erected for Ghurid patrons, within or without India.

As the case of the *kīrtimukha* demonstrates, it was not figuration *per se* that was the problem, nor even figuration in the context of mosque decoration, but the nature of what was represented in such a context. Paradoxically, despite a supposed quasi-pathological aversion to figural imagery, a surprisingly liberal attitude to figuration seems to have prevailed in the first mosques built after the Ghurid conquest.

5. Refiguring Indo-Islamic Iconoclasm

Part of the problem with the way Indo-Ghurid mosques have been conceptualized from the nineteenth-century onwards lies in a disciplinary tendency to privilege the creation of a work (be it painting, sculpture or monument) over its reception. The consequences of what might be called a synchronic fixation are abundantly clear in Cunningham's characterization of the reuse of temple materials in Ghurid mosques as a barbarous anti-aesthetic gesture. If, however, we approach the work diachronically, not as a static creation frozen at the moment of birth, but as dynamic and constantly shifting in terms of form, content and meaning, then we can begin to conceive of reuse and the role of iconoclasm in the early Indian mosque in a less reductive manner.

Far from being the driving force behind the desecration of existing monuments, such alteration of figural imagery as occurred was contingent upon a preference for the reuse of stone elements. Some of this material may have come from temples destroyed during the conquest, but the majority of it was re-deployed in a manner congruent with pre-conquest practice and seems to reflect a contemporary vogue for Indic ornament that is manifest even in the architecture of Afghanistan at this period. The various responses to figural imagery witnessed in the Indo-Ghurid mosque might be seen as a contingent compromise rooted in a tension between continuity and discontinuity. Indeed, as an architectural creation with multiple aesthetic affinities, the Indo-Ghurid mosque itself is the product of such a compromise.

In his work on iconoclasm during the French Revolution, Richard Wrigley has noted that, "in practice, we find that acts of iconoclasm are commonly exercises in compromise, usually resulting in hybridized or synthetic results" that represent a dialectical synthesis between different traditions (Wrigley 1993: 185). As Wrigley notes, the product of such compromise may be intended to convey a quite different message than the original work, but its original meanings are never entirely obliterated; they are always present under erasure, obscured yet still visible and in dialogue with the superimposed marks of effacement. Such altered images index their own history of transformation, which is integral to the production of what is in effect a new work. The act of iconoclasm may thus be seen as an attempt to re-code meaning according to new iconographic and aesthetic conventions. Rather than see the process in terms of hybridization or syncretism with its implied "condition of uneasy union" (Stewart & Ernst, forthcoming), the physical and conceptual displacements that it entails might be best conceptualized as a type of visual translation.[6] The concept of translation that it implies is not the traditional one of equivalence or fidelity to an original, however, but one closer to Derrida's notion of textual translation as "a regulated transformation of one language by another, of one text by another" (Derrida[-Bass] 1981: 20). Homi Bhabha has developed this idea in arguing that the process of translation gives rise not to secondary (and implicitly inferior) versions of original texts, but to new works that contain traces of earlier meanings that they transcend (Bhabha 1990; Evans 1994: 32). Although developed in relation to texts, this concept of translation as a transformative process that gives rise to new works has much to recommend it as a model for understanding iconoclastic transformations of existing artworks.

In a recent posthumous publication, the anthropologist Alfred Gell argued that as the product of a type of 'artistic agency', the act of iconoclasm often follows the same conceptual structure as the act of creation, giving rise to a new work, related to, but distinct from the original (Gell 1998: 62-65). The concept of the iconoclastic gesture as an extension of the creative process, a mode of creating new works out of old, has a long pedigree in western art, notably in Duchamp's *LHOOQ* (Gamboni 1997: 262), and Rauschenberg's *Erased de Kooning* (Gamboni 1997: 268). The idea of 'creative iconoclasm' has been particularly in evidence in the past decade, from which one could cite many examples. In May 1994, for example, an artist named Mark Bridger erased Damien Hirst's *Away from the Flock*, a work consisting of a whole sheep suspended in a glass tank of formaldehyde, by pouring black dye

---

6 In an important and innovative article Tony Stewart (2000) has explored the implications of different translation theories for conceptualizing inter-communal textual production in early modern Bengal. While acknowledging the value of translation theory for conceptualizing various modes of cultural production across cultural, linguistic, or religious boundaries in pre-colonial South Asia, my own theoretical perspective is more indebted to recent work located at the intersection between post-structuralist and postcolonial theories of translation (e.g. Niranjana 1992) than to formal linguistic theories.

into the solution in which the animal was suspended. Claiming authorship of the amended work, Bridger placed a label, which read "Mark Bridger, *Black Sheep*, May 1, 1994," over the original title. Sued for criminal damage, Bridger claimed that his intention was not to destroy the work but to transform it creatively (Kastner 1997: 154). The authors of the works targeted in these creative outbursts have sometimes accepted, either implicitly or explicitly, that such radical alterations to the original works constituted an extension of the creative process. Damien Hirst, for example, published an image of his *Away from the Flock* with a sliding tab that enables the reader to reproduce the inked-out version of the original work (Hirst 1997).

I do not want to suggest here that those responsible for having the figural imagery on the architectural elements reused in Indian mosques altered would have justified their actions in post-structuralist terms, if at all. Nor would I argue for a moment that they had as self-conscious or self-publicizing an approach to the act of alteration as the modern iconoclasts just mentioned. Moreover, unlike the iconoclastic gestures of French Revolutionaries or contemporary artists, the acts of iconoclasm to which Indo-Ghurid mosques bear witness were not the driving force in the production of a work that might be entitled 'The Indo-Ghurid Mosque'. They were instead *contingent* upon a decision to reuse pre-existing architectural materials, which may have constituted an attack on the religio-political symbols of the *ancien regime*, but also reflects, as we have seen, the positive aesthetic value that Afghan patrons placed on Indic art and architecture. Nevertheless, despite this difference, conceiving of iconoclastic transformation as part of a broader process of visual translation enables us to escape the bind into which we are placed when we privilege the originary work (whether Persian mosque or Indian temple) as more authentic than any subsequent work created from its elements. Transcending this synchronic fixation, we can see the physical and conceptual translations witnessed in the Indo-Ghurid mosque not as barbarous attacks upon (or crude approximations of) an originary aesthetic tradition ('Indian' or 'Persian)', but part of a process of transmutation that gave rise to the Indo-Ghurid mosque, a new work with its own distinctive aesthetic.

This analysis may seem anachronistic, but it finds some support among the Hadith discussed at the outset, which prescribe a transformative practice comparable to those just described. Among a group of Traditions that deal with the angel Gabriel's refusal to enter the house of the Prophet Muhammad is one which attributes his hesitancy to the presence of images on a curtain and another unspecified object. The remedy for the curtain is to transform it into pillows that will be thrown on the ground and trodden upon, while the Prophet is ordered to decapitate the remaining images, so that they become like trees by virtue of their inanimate status (Ibn Ḥanbal 1313/1895 2: 305, 308, 390; van Reenen 1990: 33). Formal or iconographic transformation is a relatively common response to iconoclastic concerns (witnessed, for example, in the transmutation of the Virgin into Liberty in Revolutionary France), but the nature of the transformation envisaged in the Hadith entails a radical conceptual metamorphosis. The resemblance between tree and headless image clearly lies in the fact that both are perceived to lack a spirit (*rūḥ*) and with it, the potential for animation (van Reenen 1990: 33, 54). Decapitation is evidently judged to result in the production of what are in fact images of an entirely different class than the original, inanimate and licit in place of the animate and illicit originals. The acts of desecration and creation thus appear closely intertwined, the simultaneity of their products destabilizing the boundaries between abstraction and figuration that is integral to much art historical thinking. This blurring of the boundaries is particularly marked in the iconoclastic reworking of figural material in the Ghurid mosque at Ajmer. Although the phenomenon has not been noted previously, at several points the columns in the upper levels of the southern end of the prayer-hall have had their figures removed in such a way as to leave only a rhomboid outline (figure

4), which perfectly replicates the form of the rhomboidal *ratna* designs of similar size that have been carved ex novo on the lower shafts of the same columns (figure 5). The latter replace the figural imagery normally found in this position in temple architecture (Patel 2000: 233).[7]

Both newly carved members and those that have undergone iconoclastic transformations are thus structurally and decoratively integrated in the Ajmer mosque. As Alka Patel has noted of Indo-Ghurid mosques, "if the buildings were ... viewed in their entireties, it would have been visually difficult to extract the despoliated from the newer materials" (Patel 2000: 236). The view of these mosques as disjointed reflections of the greater wholes upon whose life and death their creation is predicated probably offers more of an insight into the methodologies of modern art historians than the tastes of Ghurid patrons. At least in the case of the Delhi mosque, we have an unusual abundance of descriptions from the century and a half following its construction (Flood forthcoming). The fact that none of these thirteenth- and fourteenth-century descriptions mention either the reuse of temple elements or the associated iconoclastic alterations strongly supports the idea that the mosque was viewed as a unitary whole by those who used it.

While contingent upon a decision to reuse existing architectural elements, the alteration of figural imagery was integral to the creation of that unitary whole. A widespread and long established aversion to the use of figural imagery in the decoration of a mosque led to steps being taken to neutralize anthropomorphic images on the reused architectural elements in ways that conformed to orthodox prescriptions and established practice. The process provides evidence for the creative function of iconoclastic transformation at both the micro and the macro level: in the transformation of illicit

7 Perhaps fortuitously, the substitution of a rhomboid for anthropomorphic imagery is also found on certain late eight-century coins from Tabaristan in Iran that otherwise follow pre-Islamic numismatic models: Miles (1975): 366, pl. 25(7).

anthropomorphic figures into qualitatively new images, and in the contribution that this made to the creation of what was in effect a Ghurid *Gesamtkunstwerk*. The close relationship (in both theory and practice) between acts of image alteration and architectural creation in the early Indian mosque serves as an indication that, even when rationalized within the rhetorical frame of religious orthodoxy, iconoclasm in the medieval Islamic world was less the product of an essential cultural pathology than a series of choices made by multiple historical agents and governed by a complex nexus of aesthetic, cultural, economic, and political factors.

Bibliography

Asher, Catherine B. (2000), 'Mapping Hindu-Muslim identities through the architecture of Shahjahanabad and Jaipur', in Gilmartin, David, & Lawrence, Bruce, B. (eds.), *Beyond Turk and Hindu: Rethinking Religious Identity in Islamicate South Asia*, Gainesville: University Press of Florida, pp. 121-48.

Bahrani, Zainab (1995), 'Assault and Abduction: The Fate of the Royal Image in the Ancient Near East', *Art History*, 18 (3), September, pp. 363-82.

Ball, Warwick (1990), 'Some notes on the Masjid-i Sangi at Larwand in Central Afghanistan', *South Asian Studies*, 6, pp. 105-10.

Bhabha, Homi (1990), 'The Third Space', in Jonathan Rutherford (ed.), *Identity: Community, Culture, Difference*, London: Lawrence & Wishart.

Cunningham, Alexander (1871[-1972]), *Four Reports Made during the Years 1862-63-64-65*, Archaeological Survey of India Reports, Vol. 2, reprinted Delhi & Varanasi: Indological Book House.

Davis, Richard, H. (1992), 'Loss and recovery of ritual self among Hindu images', *Journal of Ritual Studies*, 6 (1), Winter, pp. 43-61.

________ (1997), *Lives of Indian Images*, Princeton: Princeton University Press.

Dayalan, D. (1985), 'The Role of War-Trophies in Cultural Contact', *Tamil Civilization* 3 (2-3), pp. 133-37.

Derrida, Jacques, tr. Bass, Alan (1981), *Positions*, Chicago: The University of Chicago Press.

Dhaky, M.A. (1998), *Encyclopaedia of Indian Temple Architecture, North India Beginnings of Medieval Idiom c. AD 900-1000*, New Delhi: American Institute of Indian Studies.

Dikshit, R.B.K.N. (1944), 'A Panel Showing the Birth of Lord Kṛishna from the Qutb Mosque', *The Journal of the United Provinces Historical Society*, 17 (1), pp. 84-86.

Eaton, Richard M., (2000), 'Temple Desecration and Indo-Muslim States', in Gilmartin, David, & Lawrence, Bruce, B. (eds.), *Beyond Turk and Hindu: Rethinking Religious Identity in Islamicate South Asia*, Gainesville: University Press of Florida, pp. 246-81.

Ernst, Carl., W. (2000), 'Admiring the Works of the Ancients: the ElloraTemples as Viewed by Indo-Muslim Authors', in Gilmartin, David, & Lawrence, Bruce, B. (eds.), *Beyond Turk and Hindu: Rethinking Religious Identity in Islamicate South Asia*, Gainesville: University Press of Florida, pp. 98-120.

Ettinghausen, Richard, Grabar, Oleg, & Jenkins-Madina, Marilyn (2001), *Islamic Art and Architecture 650-1250*, New Haven & London: Yale University Press.

Evans, Ruth (1994), 'Translating Past Cultures?', *The Medieval Translator*, 4, pp. 20-45.

Faris, Nabih, Amin (1952), *The Book of Idols*, Princeton: Princeton University Press.

Fine, Steven (2000), 'Iconoclasm and the Art of the Late-Ancient Palestinian Synagogues', in Levine, Lee I. and Weiss, Zeev (eds.), *From Dura to Sepphoris: Studies in Jewish Art and Society in Late Antiquity*, Portsmouth, Rhode Island.

Fischer, Klaus (1966), 'Indo-Iranian Contacts as Revealed by Mud-Brick Architecture from Afghanistan', *Oriental Art*, 12, Spring, pp. 25-29.

Flood, Finbarr Barry (2001), 'Ghūrid architecture in the Indus Valley: the Tomb of Shaykh Sādan Shahīd', *Ars Orientalis*, 31, pp. 129-66.

________ (2002), 'Between Cult and Culture: Bamiyan, Islamic Iconoclasm and the Museum', *Art Bulletin*, December.

________ (2002a), 'Between Ghazna and Delhi: Lahore and its lost *manāra*', in Ball, Warwick and Harrow, Leonard (eds.), *Cairo to Kabul: Afghan and Islamic Studies Presented to Ralph Pinder-Wilson*, London: Melisende, pp. 102-12.

________ (forthcoming), *Incorporating India: Objects and Others in a Medieval Transcultural Polity*.

Flood, Finbarr Barry (unpublished), 'Transcribing Ruins, Inscribing Difference: Architectural Photography as Ethnographic Practice in Colonial India', unpublished paper presented to the South Asia Program of Cornell University (Spring 2000), and to *Photography in the Islamic World 19th-20th Centuries*, a one-day symposium held at Harvard University (December 2000).

Freedberg, David (1989), *The Power of Images: Studies in the History and Theory of Response*, Chicago & London: The University of Chicago Press.

Gamboni, Dario (1997), *The Destruction of Art: Iconoclasm and Vandalism since the French Revolution*, New Haven: Yale University Press.

Gell, Alfred (1998), *Art and Agency: an Anthropological Theory*, Oxford: Clarendon Press.

Goel, Sita Ram (1993), *Hindu Temples: What Happened to Them? Vol. 2: The Islamic Evidence*, 2nd enlarged edition, New Delhi: Voice of India.

Golzio, Karl-Heinz (1990), 'Das Problem von Toleranz in Indischen Relgionen anhand epigraphischer Quellen', in Eimer, Helmut (ed.), *Frank-Richard Hamm Memorial Volume, October 8, 1990*, Bonn: Indica et Tibetica Verlag, pp. 89-102.

Grabar, Oleg (1977), 'Islam and Iconoclasm', in Bryer, Anthony, & Herrin, Judith (eds.), *Iconoclasm. Papers given at the Ninth Spring Symposium of Byzantine Studies, University of Birmingham, March 1975*, Birmingham: Centre for Byzantine Studies, University of Birmingham, pp. 45-52.

________ (1987), *The Formation of Islamic Art*, New Haven: Yale University Press.

Gregory, Andrew, P. (1994), '"Powerful Image": Responses to Portraits and the Political Uses of Images in Rome', *Journal of Roman Archaeology*, 7, pp. 80-99.

Grover, Satish (1981), *The Architecture of India: Islamic (727-1707 AD)*, New Delhi: Vikas Publishing House.

Guha-Thakurta, Tapati (1997), *Archaeology as Evidence: Looking Back from the Ayodhya Debate*, Calcutta: Centre for Studies in Social Sciences.

Hawting, G.R. (1999), *The Idea of Idolatry and the Emergence of Islam: From Polemic to History*, Cambridge: Cambridge University Press.

Hillenbrand, Robert (1988), 'Political Symbolism in Early Indo-Islamic Mosque Architecture: The Case of Ajmīr', *Iran*, 26, 105-17.

Hirst, Damien (1997), *I Want to Spend the Rest of My Life Everywhere, with Everyone, One to One, Always, Forever, Now*, New York: Monacelli Press.

Horovitz, J. (1911-12), 'The Inscriptions of Muḥammad ibn Sām, Quṭbuddin Aibeg and Iltutmish', *Epigraphia Indo-Moslemica*, pp. 12-34.

Ibn Ḥanbal, Aḥmad (1313/1895), *Musnad*, 6 vols., Cairo.

Jacoby, Zehava (1992), 'Ideological and Pragmatic Aspects of Muslim Iconoclasm After the Crusader Advent in the Holy Land', in Michalski, Sergiusz (ed.), *L'Art et les révolutions, Section 4: Les iconoclasmes*, Actes du XXVIIe congrès international d'histoire de l'art, Strasbourg 1-7 septembre 1989, Strasbourg: Société alsacienne pour le dévelopment de l'histoire de l'art, pp. 13-24.

Kastner, Jeffrey (1997), 'Art Attack', *ARTnews*, October, pp. 154-56.

Kinney, Dale (1995), 'Rape or Restitution of the Past? Interpreting *Spolia*', *Papers in Art History from the Penn. State University*, 9, pp. 53-67.

Kumar, Sunil, 'Qutb and Modern Memory', in Kaul, Suvir (ed.), *The Partitions of Memory: The Afterlife of the Division of India*, New Delhi: Permanent Black, pp. 140-82.

Lehmann, Fritz (1978), 'The Name and Origin of the Aṭāla Masjid, Jaunpur', *Islamic Culture*, 52, pp. 19-27.

Meister, Michael (1972), 'The "Two-and-a-half-day" Mosque', *Oriental Art*, N.S. 18/1, pp. 57-63.

________ (1993), 'Indian Islam's Lotus Throne: Kaman and Khatu Kalan', in Anna Libera Dallapiccola & Stephanie Zingel-Avé Lallemant (eds.), *Islam and Indian Regions*, Stuttgart: Franz Steiner Verlag, pp. 445-52.

Miles, G.C. (1975), 'Numismatics', *The Cambridge History of Iran*, Vol. 4: The Period from the Arab Invasions to the Saljuqs, Cambridge: Cambridge University Press, pp. 364-77.

Niranjana, Tejaswini (1992), *Siting Translation: History, Post-Structuralism and the Colonial Context*, Berkeley & Los Angeles: University of California Press.

Page, J.A. (1926), *An Historical Memoir on the Qutb: Delhi*, Memoirs of the Archaeological Survey of India, no. 22, Calcutta: Government of India Central Publication Branch.

Paret, Rudi (1960), 'Textbelege zum islamische Bilderverbot', in *Das Werk des Künstlers: Studien zur Ikonographie und formgeschichte Hubert Schrade zum 60. Geburtstag dargebracht von Kollegen und Schülern*, Stuttgart: W. Kohlhammer Verlag, pp. 36-48.

_______ (1968), 'Das Islamische Bilderverbot und die Schia', in Gräf, Erwin (ed.), *Festschrift Werner Caskel. Zum siebzigsten Geburtstag 5. März 1966 Gewidmet von freunden und Schülern*, Leiden: Brill, pp. 224-32.

_______ (1976-77), 'Die Entstehungszeit des Islamischen Bilderverbots', *Kunst des Orients*, 11 (1-2), pp. 158-79.

Patel, Alka A. (2000), *Islamic Architecture of Western India (mid-12th-14th Centuries): Continuities and Interpretations*, unpublished D.Phil. thesis, Harvard University.

Pedersen, J. (1991), 'Masdjid', *The Encyclopaedia of Islam*, new edition, Vol. 6, pp. 644-77.

Petrosyan, Yuri, A., Akimushkin, Oleg, F., Khalidov, Anad, B., Rezvan, & Efim, A. (1995), *Pages of Perfection: Islamic Paintings and Calligraphy from the Russian Academy of Sciences*, St. Petersburg, Milan:Electa.

Pinder-Wilson, Ralph (2001), 'Ghaznavid and Ghūrid Minarets', *Iran*, 39, pp. 155-86.

Pope, Arthur, Upham (1946), 'Representations of Living Forms in Persian Mosques', *Bulletin of the Iranian Institute*, 6 (1), pp. 125-29.

Roux, Jean-Paul (1980), 'Mosquées Anatoliennes a décor sculpté', *Syria*, 57, pp. 305-23.

Said, Hakim Mohammad (1410/1989), tr., *Al-Beruni's Book on Mineralogy: The Book Most Comprehensive in Knowledge on Precious Stones*, Islamabad: Pakistan Hijra Council.

Sastri, Hirananda (1937), 'Devanāgarī and the Muhammadan Rulers of India', *Journal of the Bihar and Orissa Research Society*, 23, pp. 492-97.

Scarcia, Gianroberto, & Taddei, Maurizio (1973), 'The Masjid-i sangī of Larvand', *East and West*, N.S. 23, pp. 89-108.

Schick, Robert (1995), *The Christian Communities of Palestine from Byzantine to Islamic Rule: A Historical and Archaeological Study*, Studies in Late Antiquity and Early Islam, 2, Princeton: The Darwin Press, Inc.

Shokoohy, Mehrdad (1988), *Bhadreśvar, the Oldest Islamic Monuments in India*, Leiden: E.J. Brill.

Shokoohy, Mehrdad & Shokoohy, Natalie H. (1987), 'The Architecture of Baha al-Din Tughrul in the Region of Bayana, Rajasthan', *Muqarnas*, 4, pp. 114-32.

________ (1993), *Nagaur: Sultanate and Early Mughal History and Architecture of the District of Nagaur, India*, London: Royal Asiatic Society.

________ (1996), 'Indian Subcontinent III, 6(iii)(b): 11th-16th Century Indo-Islamic Architecture: North', *Dictionary of Art*, Vol. 15, New York: MacMillan Publishing Limited, pp. 338-46.

________ (2000), 'The Karao Jāmi' Mosque of Diu in the Light of the History of the Island', *South Asian Studies*, 16, pp. 55-72.

Stewart, Tony K. (2000), 'In Search of Equivalence: Conceiving Hindu-Muslim Encounter Through Translation Theory', *History of Religions* 40 (3), pp. 260-87.

Stewart, Tony & Ernst, Carl (forthcoming), 'Syncretism', in Claus, Peter J. & Mills, Margaret A. (eds.), *South Asian Folklore: An Encyclopedia*, New York: Garland Publishing Inc.

Thapar, Romila (1994), *Cultural Transaction and Early India: Tradition and Patronage*, Delhi: Oxford University Press.

van Reenen, Daan (1990), 'The *Bilderverbot*, a new survey', *Der Islam*, 67, pp. 27-77.

Wagoner, Phillip B., & Rice, John Henry (2001), 'From Delhi to the Deccan: Newly Discovered Tughluq Monuments at Warangal-Sulṭānpūr and the Beginnings of Indo-Islamic Architecture in Southern India', *Artibus Asiae*, 31/1, pp. 77-117.

Welch (1993), 'Architectural Patronage and the Past: the Tughluq Sultans of Delhi', *Muqarnas*, 10, pp. 311-22.

Wensinck, A.J. [-Fahd, T.] (1997), 'Ṣura 1. In Theological and Legal Doctrine', *The Encyclopedia of Islam*, new edition, Vol. 9, pp. 889-92.

Wink, André (1997), *Al Hind, the Making of the Indo-Islamic World, Vol. 2: The Slave Kings and the Islamic Conquest 11th-13th Centuries*, New Delhi: Oxford University Press.

Wrigley, Richard (1993), 'Breaking the Code: Interpreting French Revolutionary Iconoclasm', in Yarrington, Alison, & Everest, Kelvin (eds.), *Reflections of Revolution, Images of Romanticism*, New York & London: Routledge, pp. 182-95.

1. Chaurasi Khamba Mosque, Kaman, defaced reused capital.

2. Qutbi Mosque, Delhi, decapitated figures on reused pillar.

3. Qutbi mosque, Delhi, reused pilasters with *kīrtimukha* figure intact while the *apsaras* emerging from its mouth have been defaced.

4. Arhai-din-ka Jhompra Mosque, Ajmer, erased figure with rhomboidal outline.

5. Arhai-din-ka Jhompra Mosque, Ajmer, corresponding pillar with *ratna* design.

APPENDIX

A Translation of Former Prime Minister Atal Bihari Vajpayee's Address to the Public Meeting at Somnath*

New Delhi, Kartik, 1923
31, October, 2001

The following is the text [in Hindi] of the speech made by the Prime Minister, Shri Atal Bihari Vajpayee, today, at Somnath (Gujarat) on the occasion of the golden jubilee of the 'Sanctification of the *jyotirlinga* at Somnath'.

Today is a day of great joy. Today it is exactly fifty years since the idol of Lord Somnath was sanctified here at the temple. There is another reason for joy – today is also the *jayanti* of Sardar Vallabhbhai Patel. This is his 125th anniversary. This is a precious coincidence – like the invaluable union of gold and diamond – for had Sardar not been there Somnath would not exist today in this form. In what state it would have existed I cannot say. But Somnath is the symbol of our *sanatan sanskriti* (timeless culture), our *shaswat dharma* (eternal religion, way of life), the symbol of the successive shifts and changes in our history. History had also witnessed that moment when conquering invaders razed Somnath to the ground. Today too such tendencies are becoming stronger. But the manner in which we resurrected Somnath, rebuilt Somnath on new foundations, and defeated the ones who razed it to the ground and destroyed it – in the same manner those who want to advance on

* The text was officially made available to media by the Government agencies.

the strength of terrorism today, who do not worship idols but want to destroy them, these people will meet the same fate as those who had dared to break Somnath [in the past]. Somnath is the symbol of our immortal culture, Somnath is the symbol of that continuing struggle, Somnath is the symbol of our national self-respect.

Today Lord Somnath is being well cared for. Pilgrims come here from all over the country. This is a matter of great joy. We want that Somnath and the entire neighbourhood around it should gain a new life, a new form. There are a number of pilgrimage centres close to Somnath, which are linked with it but are spread out in the region. Here we have Porbunder, here we have many holy places for the immersion of ashes, and here we have the picturesque Giri, a place worth visiting. There is Palitana, there is Junagadh, and I can see before me Somnath in the past repeatedly razed to the ground and still standing tall, talking with the sky. Standing proud exactly at the same spot where so many unsuccessful attempts were made to destroy its pride. In this region we now have a new Chief Minister, and I am convinced that he will make efforts towards enhancing this sacred space [around Somnath]. Whatever resources are required for this would be somewhat taken care of by the Indian Government. Listen to this carefully – you may understand 'somewhat' to mean just a little or you may understand it to mean all that is required. It all depends on your perception. But this region is a sacred space. Dwarika is here, and I have already mentioned Palitana. Gujarati tourists travel in very large numbers to other parts of the state; they travel to all parts of the country. In the same measure tourists residing in other parts of the country should visit Gujarat. It is very necessary to ensure that. I have been told that there is one difficulty – there is no broad gauge [railway track]. This drawback was noticed even when Advaniji decided to begin his *yatra* from here on a *rath* rather than by train! Of course he had anyway made up his mind to travel on his *rath*, but a broad gauge for railways must be established here – of that I am convinced, and a broad gauge will most definitely be built here, I assure you of that.

Gujarat has immense possibilities for growth and development, although it is true that Gujarat has had to face a lot of adversity due to nature — such a massive earthquake. But I want to congratulate the people of Gujarat, of Kutch, to thank them for the courage with which they have faced the natural calamities. A new Kutch, a new Gujarat is being built out of the fallen ruins. I remember the day when people came (from distant places) offering help, and the self-respecting people who were no doubt in need, but had their pride intact, would say that they did not need help. We can stand up on our own; we do not require anybody's help. In those days we even saw another side of the rest of the world; it seemed the whole world partook in alleviating problems, wherever a crisis loomed. Differences were forgotten. Petty conflicts were overlooked. Before the earthquake there were the floods, the drought; Gujarat has been in continuous struggle with nature. But mankind has never accepted defeat in the face of the challenges from nature. For this I want to congratulate the people of Gujarat. You may go anywhere in the world, to any part of the world, you will find migrants from Gujarat. They will meet you with great affection, and if you are a little confused about the food offered, the minute you taste the sweet *daal* (lentils) you will immediately recognize that it is Gujarati food you are being offered. Such sweetness, one sometimes thinks had there been a bit of sourness as well it would be to advantage. Perhaps Narendra bhai [Narendra Modi, the Chief Minister of Gujarat] can inject that. Hard work needs this edge, the confidence to move forward, the resolve to meet all challenges. Such resolve that was the hallmark of Sardar Patel's life; had Sardar not been there, there would have been no Bharat. The British wanted to divide Bharat into 500 pieces (separate regions) before they actually left. The rajas and nawabs of that time were dreaming of ruling over each of these separate kingdoms. People were saying Bharat would get divided. Sardar said "No"; the division we have agreed to is correct, but there will be no more divisions. Whether Kashmir should remain here or whether it should be there – whenever there are such discussions people forget (Sardar Patel), and Advaniji has referred to this recently – the people of Jammu and Kashmir had voluntarily opted to be a part of Bharat, that decision cannot be reversed, that pledge is unbreakable, that decision is unchangeable. We will not allow the country to be divided again. That it happened once was unfortunate, there was foreign rule, the design to create divisions; but Sardar was there, and under his leadership the foundation of national unity was created. He brought together all the small and big kingdoms and gave Bharat its form of a grand nation.

Today Bharat is strong, today Bharat is organized, today Bharat is moving forward towards prosperity. Today Bharat is ready to face any challenge. Nobody should be under an illusion. Some people fall prey to illusions when they see our sisters adorned with bangles, and they cite those bangles.† We don't speak such a language. But we do say that in Punjab, where wearing bangles is a custom, where the practice is widespread and with reference to which this has been said – along with bangles a *karha* (wrist-band) is also worn, a *karha* made of iron. Bangles along with the *karha* – but it is not an indication of manliness to keep harping on bangles. Maintaining our self-control and keeping our armed forces on alert, having confidence in our scientists and congratulating our soldiers – all that Sardar Patel has bequeathed to us as heritage – we will defend it and move forward. I have confidence that this region will develop and move forward. If there are any new schemes in the offing we will sit with the Chief Minister and discuss them.

I am very grateful for the opportunity to be here today and express my veneration to Lord Somnath. Namaskar!

---

† The Prime Minister was referring to a common slight to male masculinity where it was suggested that a man adorned himself, like a woman, with bangles. He reminded his audience that in the Punjab men wear the *karha*, an iron wrist band, and nobody (at least not since the British invented the idea of 'martial races') would dare cast aspersions on Punjabi masculinity.

A Select Bibliography of recent publications on 'Hindu-Muslim' Relations in Pre-Modern India

Ahmad, Aziz, 'Epic and Counter Epic in Medieval India', *Journal of the American Oriental Society*, vol. 83 (1963), pp. 470–76.

Alam, Muzaffar, 'Assimilation from a Distance: Confrontation and Sufi Accomodation in Awadh Society', in R. Champaklakshmi and S. Gopal, ed., *Tradition, Dissent and Ideology: Essays in Honour of Romila Thapar* (Delhi: Oxford University Press, 1996).

Alam, Muzaffar, 'Competition and Co-existence: Indo-Islamic Interaction in Medieval North India', *Itinerario*, vol. 13 (1989), pp. 37–59.

Alam, Muzaffar, *The Political Language of Islam* (Delhi: Permanent Black, 2004).

Amin, Shahid, 'On Retelling the Muslim Conquest of North India' in Partha Chatterjee and Anjan Ghosh, ed., *History and the Present* (Delhi: Permanent Black, 2002).

Bayly, Christopher A., '"The Pre-History of Communalism"? Religious Conflict in India, 1700-1860', *Modern Asian Studies*, vol. 19 (1985), pp. 177–203.

Chattopadhyay, Brajadulal, *Representing the Other? Sanskrit Sources and the Muslims (Eighth to Fourteenth Century)* (Delhi: Manohar, 1998).

Dalmia, Vasudha and H. von Stietencron, *Representing Hinduism: The Construction of Religious Traditions and National Identity* (New Delhi: Sage Publications, 1995).

Das, Veena, *Mirrors of Violence: Communities, Riots and Survivors in South Asia (*Delhi: Oxford University Press, 1990).

Eaton, Richard, ed. *India's Islamic Traditions, 711–1750* (Delhi: Oxford University Press, Oxford in India Readings, 2003).

Eaton, Richard, *Essays on Islam and Indian History* (Delhi: Oxford University Press, 2001 reprint).

Eaton, Richard, *The Rise of Islam and the Bengal Frontier, 1204–1760* (Delhi: Oxford University Press, 1997 reprint).

Ernst, Carl W.. *The Eternal Garden: Mysticism, History and Politics at a South Asian Sufi Center* (Albany: State University of New York Press, 1992).

Flood, F. Barry, 'Between Cult and Culture: Bamiyan, Islamic Iconoclasm, and the Museum', *The Art Bulletin*, 84 (2002), pp. 641–59.

Gilmartin, David and Bruce B.Lawrence, eds., *Beyond Turk and Hindu: Rethinking Religious Identities in Islamicate South Asia* (Gainesville: University Press of Florida, 2000).

Gopal, S, *Anatomy of a Confrontation: the Babri Masjid-Ram Janmabhumi Issue (*Delhi, 1991).

Habib, Mohammad, 'Mahmud of Ghazni', in *Politics and Society during the Early Medieval Period, Collected Works of Professor Habib, vol. 2* (Delhi: People's Publishing House, 1981), pp. 36–104.

Habib, Muhammad, 'Introduction to Elliot and Dowson's History of India vol. II', *Politics and Society during the Early Medieval Period, Collected Works of Professor Habib*, vol. 1 (Delhi: People's Publishing House, 1974), pp. 33–110.

Kumar, Sunil, *The Present in Delhi's Pasts* (Delhi: Three Essays Collective, 2008).

Lorenzen, David N., 'Who Invented Hinduism?', *Comparative Studies in Society and History*, vol. 41 (1999), pp. 630–59.

Ludden, David, *Making India Hindu: Religious Community, and the Politics of Democracy in India* (Delhi: Oxford University Press, second edition, 2005).

Mayaram, Shail, *Resisting Regimes: Myth, Memory and the Shaping of a Muslim Identity* (Delhi: Oxford University Press, 1997).

Mayaram, Shail, 'Rethinking Meo Identity: Cultural Faultline, Syncretism, Hybridity or Liminality', *Comparative Studies of South Asia, Africa and the Middle East*, vol. 17 (1997), pp. 35–45.

Metcalf, Barbara D., 'Presidential Address: Too Little and Too Much. Reflections on Muslims in the History of India', *Journal of Asian Studies*, vol. 54 (1995), pp. 951-67.

Pandey, Gyanendra, *Hindus and Others: the Question of Identity in India Today* (Delhi: Oxford University Press, 1993).

Pollock, Sheldon, 'Ramayana and Political Imagination in India', *Journal of Asian Studies*, vol. 52 (1993), pp. 261–297.

Phukan, Shantanu, '"Through throats where many rivers meet": the Ecology of Hindi in the world of Persian', *Indian Economic and Social History Review,* 38 (2001), pp. 33–58.

Richards, John F., 'The Islamic Frontier in the East: Expansion into South Asia', *South Asia*, vol. 4 (1974), pp. 91–109.

Schimmel, Annemarie, 'Turk and Hindu: a Poetical Image and its Application to Historical Fact'. In S. Vrynonis, ed., *Islam and Cultural Change in the Middle Ages* (Wiesbaden: Otto Haarassowitz, 1975), pp. 107–26.

Sontheimer, Günther D. and Hermann Kulke, eds. *Hinduism Reconsidered* (Delhi: Manohar, 1989).

Sreenivasan, Ramya, 'Alauddin Khalji Remembered: Conquest, Gender and Community in Medieval Rajput Narratives', *Studies in History*, ns 18 (2002), pp. 275–96.

Subrahmanyam, Sanjay, 'Before the Leviathan: Sectarian Violence and State in pre-colonial India', in Kaushik Basu and Sanjay Subrahmanyam, eds., *Unravelling the Nation: Sectarian Conflict and India's Secular Identity* (Delhi: Penguin Books, 1996).

Subrahmanyam, Sanjay, 'Violence and Identities in South Asia: Grievance and Memory in Community Formation', *Purusartha*, vol. 22 (2001), pp. 47–70.

Talbot, Cynthia, 'Inscribing the Other, Inscribing the Self: Hindu-Muslim Identities in Pre-Colonial India', *Comparative Studies in Society and History*, vol. 37 (1995), pp. 692–722.

Thapar, Romila, *Cultural Pasts: Essays in Early Indian History* (Delhi: Oxford University Press, 2000).

Thapar, Romila, *Somanatha: the Many Voices of a History* (Delhi: Viking/Penguin, 2004).

Wagoner, Philip B. and John H. Rice, 'From Delhi to the Deccan: Newly Discovered Tughluq Monuments at Warangal-Sultanpur and the beginnings of Indo-Islamic architecture in southern India', *Artibus Asiae*, 61 (2001), pp. 77–117.

Wagoner, Phillip B., '"Sultan among Hindu Kings": Dress, Titles, and the Islamicization of Hindu Culture at Vijayanagara', *Journal of Asian Studies*, vol. 55 (1996), pp. 851–880.